HAPPINESS

The Art of Micro-Actions

Nancy Freedman

Happiness: The Art of Micro-Actions

nancyfreedman.com

Published by Made to Change the World™ Publishing
Nashville, TN

ISBN: 978-1-956837-48-3 Print
      978-1-956837-49-0 ebook

Printed in the USA, Canada, Australia, and Europe

To you:

- The young woman who seeks direction.

- The friend and sister who wishes to be there in the best and worst times.

- The daughter pulled between personal desires and feelings of responsibility.

- The mother who desires the best for her children.

- The wife who tirelessly supports her spouse.

To each and every one of you who has lost your happiness to chaos and overwhelm: May the practices in this book—practices that I learned and earned through my own life experiences—serve you to find genuine happiness in the micro-moments once again.

CONTENTS

ACKNOWLEDGMENTS

My biggest thanks goes to all of you, the women who are juggling and working to create happiness for those around them and for themselves— thank you for being my inspiration, for giving me the motivation that has pushed me forward to share.

Thank you to **Tony Robbins** and **Dean Graziosi** for the positive influences that you have had on my life.

Thank you to **Ellie Shefi** and the entire **Made to Change the World Publishing** team for your insight and guidance in putting ideas on paper.

Thank you to the strong women that have been role models for both strength and femininity and who have encouraged my personal growth in life. Thank you particularly to **Sage Robbins** who demonstrates this so beautifully.

Thank you to the **best girl friends** a woman could ask for, who always know how to support me and bring out all the best feminine qualities in me exactly when I need them.

And of course, a special thank you to my whole family, who have patiently and lovingly supported me throughout the process of sharing these messages with you.

INTRODUCTION

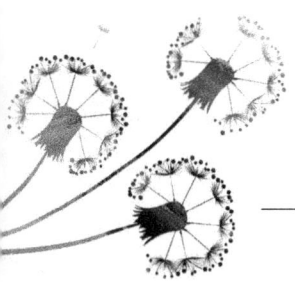

> *It's not easy to find happiness in ourselves,*
> *and it's not possible to find it elsewhere.*
> — AGNES REPPLIER

I have always strived to find a way to be the best that I can be. But life is a journey. There have been highs and there have been lows. I have been happy and I have been unhappy. And I know that I will experience unhappiness again. It is what makes me grow.

But I also know that I have experienced genuine happiness in the most ordinary moments. In my quiet moments of reflection, I realized that it had been in the moments when I was intentional about viewing happiness as a *practice* and not as a state to be achieved, that I felt happiness. This realization was my moment of clarity. This was my awakening.

For most of my life, I believed that happiness came from achieving the perfect balance—a state of equilibrium where everything in life aligned, and I would never feel dissatisfied again. But as it turns out, this is an illusion, and waiting for everything to fall into place before you start experiencing happiness only leads to frustration. Instead, I realized that happiness is not a static state but a series of intentional actions that allow you to experience joy in the present moment—even when life feels heavy, scary, or uncertain.

Like you, I have endured experiences that turned my world upside down. I have felt overwhelmed, lost, and afraid. At my lowest point, I found myself suddenly widowed, and my husband's death forced me into uncharted emotional territory, pushing me to grow in ways I never imagined. Through this experience, I came to realize that happiness is not something we find, it is something we create.

I am not here to teach you how to do it all. Instead, I am here to share with you ways to create happiness no matter what. This book is about realizing that you have the power to cultivate happiness—at any time, in any place, and in any circumstances—through your actions. Happiness is a mindset shift and a daily practice that requires regular attention. Experiencing happiness requires that you take simple yet powerful micro-actions in every area of your life—and the information in this book will show you how.

PART
ONE

THE TOOLS

You are likely juggling many responsibilities in your life at the moment—responsibilities as a parent, child, employee, boss, friend, partner, and overall good human. Looking at everything at once can feel overwhelming. The true secret to happiness lies in intentionally focusing on each individual area of your life and taking the necessary micro-actions to change what needs to be changed in that area so that you can move toward cultivating happiness.

While we often seek happiness from external validation or accomplishment, happiness is internal. And finding lasting happiness starts with self-understanding. It is essential to be honest with yourself about where you are now, what you really want, what your priorities truly are in this season of your life, and what assumptions you carry with you into every relationship and space you operate in. Once you are clear on these things, you will be able to see how they shape your experience of the world around you.

True happiness is something that is available to you at any stage of your life; it is a choice you make. It can be fostered by focusing on intentional micro-actions that help you manage your priorities and move toward the life you want to live, even when experiencing unimaginable hardship.

This book is designed to meet you where you are right now and is also created for you to return to again and again as you need, to rediscover new wisdom, and to refocus on what needs your attention as you travel life's path. The set of tools I am going to share with you is not a one-off fix for finding happiness, but a philosophy and practice you will live by. You can download worksheets, prompts, and helpful exercises for each area of your life at *nancysfreetools.com*. There, you'll find folders containing tools to support you as you work through each chapter.

The first tool that is going to help you on your journey is the "Seven Happiness Practices," which are discussed in detail later in Part One—so be sure to start there. Every chapter includes the "Happiness Practices" for success in that particular area of your life, but you can use any of the "Practices" at any stage. When doing the work in a particular area, refer back to the "Happiness Practices" that are recommended for that chapter to help guide you. The "Practices" are designed to take you beneath the surface of your life and reveal unhelpful thoughts, behaviors, and assumptions that may be holding you back from experiencing true happiness.

The next tool in this journey is called the "Wheel of Life," available at *nancysfreetools.com*. Once you have an understanding of the "Happiness Practices," and before moving on to Part Two of this book, be sure to download and complete the "Wheel of Life." It will help you assess your current state and identify which areas of your life need your attention. This tool will help you identify your strengths and determine where there is room for growth. Each area of your life is represented by a segment in the wheel, and each segment has a corresponding chapter in this book. You do not have to start at Chapter 1 or read this book in order from cover to cover!

Each chapter is designed to stand on its own so you can start anywhere based on your own personal priorities and the areas of your life you'd like to focus on. And don't forget to take advantage of the free resources for each chapter, found at *nancysfreetools.com*. Be sure to come back to chapters over time as life changes and as you grow!

Remember, some areas will require greater focus at one time or another. What was a strength before may be a weaker area now, and as your focus shifts, what previously appeared as a weakness may become a strength.

The most effective way forward is to determine your priorities and start with the essential micro-actions first. To do this, you need to be as honest as possible. You won't be sharing your answers to any questions with anyone, so you don't need to be afraid of what others will think of you. The more honest you are with yourself, the clearer you will be on the areas of the wheel that need your attention.

Once you've identified which areas need the most attention, you can prioritize them and then move on to Part Two of this book. Work through the chapters in order of your priorities (based on your "Wheel of Life"), and then apply the "Continuum Tool." This tool is designed to help you intentionally take action to change what you are doing in your life right now, and through these changes, cultivate happiness in your life.

The "Continuum Tool" is a fancy name for a relatively straightforward writing assignment. You will chart a path to shift your focus to where you are going and document the details to help you outline the micro-actions that you need to take to get there. Each chapter starts with a short explanation of the "Continuum Tool" and how to apply it to that chapter. You will find the "Continuum Tool" at *nancysfreetools.com*. Be sure to download it.

It's no secret that we, as humans, tend to move away from pain and toward pleasure, and the "Continuum Tool" can help you better understand your direction. Simply put, this tool creates a vision for what you are moving away from and what you are moving toward. However, to do that, you need to know where you are now. So, this tool has four steps. Be sure to follow these four steps when you are using the "Continuum Tool."

STEP ONE asks you to describe the area of your life you have chosen to focus on based on your "Wheel of Life." For example, let's say your chosen area was "Exercise." You will write a paragraph about what exercise looks like. Be as detailed as possible, and remember to be honest. This part is not about a vision; it is about reality. For example, *I like the idea of exercising, but I hate to do it alone, so I often skip the activity unless my friends are available.*

Then note what you like and don't like about exercise. For example, *I love meeting my friends for a bike ride, but my favorite part is socializing with them at the coffee shop afterward. I want to participate in a bike race but can't get stronger. I want to use the stationary bike, but I only do it once a week for twenty minutes before I get bored.* You should also include a very concrete example of your actual routine. That might consist of which days you exercise, what exercise you do, and how long you do it for. Since honesty is key, be sure to also include the things you do less often! Ultimately, you are working to retrain your brain to move away from a painful image and closer to a positive image. Step Two is about creating a positive image.

STEP TWO is the most fun, but I caution you to make it realistic and attainable. Having a vision of greatness in any area is fantastic, but make sure it is compatible with your life.

In the exercise example, Step Two asks you to imagine how you might feel about exercise in the future. You will need to project to the future and consider what the best-case scenario in this area looks like. Are you on a cycle tour through Europe? Are you winning a race? How has your perspective of exercise changed with your best-case scenario? Now, look back at your likes and dislikes. Are those still the same in your future scenario, or have there been any changes?

Here, you're creating a positive future, a pleasurable one, and something that makes you feel happy when imagining it. This vision will move you toward pleasure. This is your best-case scenario if you are brave enough to take micro-actions in this area.

STEP THREE is designed to give you some perspective. Ask yourself what your life will look like if you don't take micro-actions in this area. This might be more challenging because it asks you to consider the worst-case scenario. What will happen if I don't take any micro-actions in this area? What if I start to do less than I am currently doing? What will happen if I focus less on this area? This is designed to provide you with some emotional pain.

Using the exercise example, this might include stopping meeting your friends since it takes so much time, and now, you lose exercise and your friendships. This lack of activity snowballs and means you lose some muscle tone, which leads to an injury that prevents you from doing any other activities for some time. This continues to spiral until your exercise is limited to walking to the mailbox. Of course, this is a dramatic picture, but the reality is that such a downward spiral isn't uncommon.

Creating this negative image for yourself can be the pain you want to avoid and the motivation you need to take micro-actions. You are trying to avoid pain, and that will move you forward. So, create a dramatic image to focus on. Build the image in your mind so vividly that you can see yourself with a cane or a broken ankle or in the worst situation relative to the area of life.

STEP FOUR is creating micro-actions that take you from where you are to where you want to be. Progress—not perfection—is the ultimate goal, so micro-actions are your friend. Each chapter in this book will offer suggestions and ideas for micro-actions to move you forward in each area of your life. Use the "Happiness Practices" to guide you. And don't forget that there is a library of free tools to support you as you work through each section of the book. If you haven't already done so, be sure to download them at *nancysfreetools.com*. The tips, tools, prompts, and exercises will support your self-reflection and growth.

THE IMPORTANCE
OF GOALS AND
CREATING
A PLAN

Now that you know where you want to be—and what will happen if you do nothing—let's focus on how you can create a plan to move forward. Download the "Goals," "Scheduling," and "Habits" resources available at *nancysfreetools.com* to dive more deeply into how you can develop a plan for success once you have prioritized each area of your "Wheel of Life" and reflected on the scenarios with the "Continuum Tool." Come back to this reminder each time you start work in one of the areas of your life.

A successful plan consists of three elements:

    1. Goals   2. Scheduling   3. Habits

Your goals are the outcome you want to achieve in that area of your life. Using the "Wheel of Life" and "Continuum Tool," you will clarify your goals, which will create a guiding vision—like a lighthouse— helping you determine your next steps.

However, big goals can seem overwhelming and unattainable, and this is often why we fail to follow-through on achieving them. Breaking your big goals into manageable micro-actions will make them easier to accomplish.

With clear goals in mind, you can reverse-engineer a path to achieve them. Outline what you need to do daily, monthly, weekly, and even yearly to get there. Once you have clarity on these micro-actions, create a schedule to allocate time for them. Start by documenting how you currently spend your time, down to the minute. Once you recognize how you currently spend your time, it will be much easier to reorganize your time to include your new micro-actions.

Life is busy and without intentional planning, you are setting yourself up to fail. Scheduling is key to implementing your new micro-actions and ensuring your long-term success. Once you have an in-depth view of how you spend your time daily, weekly, monthly, and yearly, you will eliminate any excuses you have about "not enough time." This will make it much easier to make an honest commitment to yourself and hold yourself accountable to the new micro-actions you are taking. It will take active effort and consistency—which may be difficult or uncomfortable at first—but remember, in time and with consistency, your micro-actions will lead to powerful changes that will help you actively design a life that makes you happy.

Over time, you will be able to start stacking micro-actions together, which will lead to the development of new habits. Building new habits is typically easier than trying to undo an already existing habit that no longer serves you. Some of these old habits will be the excuses you are tempted to make when trying to build momentum, so make sure you know what they are and be willing to challenge yourself when they arise!

Consider using one of these methods to make the process of building new habits easier. Try **tacking** a new micro-action onto an old habit to remind yourself and to allow you to remain consistent. Or try **tweaking** an existing habit by making a small change to it that takes you in the direction of your goal rather than suddenly cutting it out completely.

It's important to recognize that emotions play an important role when implementing new micro-actions and forming new habits. These emotions can be significant factors in your decision-making process, sometimes overriding logic or your conscious mind. Not letting your emotions take you out of the game is one of the many reasons you need to understand your motivation for doing this work, which the "Continuum Tool" will help you unpack.

Goal setting, scheduling, and building habits can feel like hard work. Instead of trying to change your whole life, take the first step toward making a change in one area of your life. If you need help with this, use the free downloadable tools and resources available at *nancysfreetools.com*.

DON'T BEAT YOURSELF UP!

When you are honest with yourself, looking at everything you need to work on may feel overwhelming, but it can also be empowering. If it feels overwhelming, be gentle with yourself. Remember that change takes time. But this book empowers you with the tools and micro-actions you need to progress toward the happiness you seek! You are learning how to apply the "Happiness Practices" to each area of your life and you are becoming an active creator of your happiness! No more being a helpless bystander watching your life unfold. Celebrate every micro-action you take because it's the small but powerful steps taken consistently that transform how you live—inside and out. Just recognizing what areas need work is a crucial micro-action, so start by celebrating yourself for being here!

Celebrating trains your brain to recognize your progress and helps you to stay focused on your wins. It's no secret that comparison kills happiness, so training your brain to focus on your progress and the wins you are experiencing helps keep the focus where it needs to be—on your own life. Don't let looking at other people's lives rob you of your happiness. Remember, everyone has challenges (no matter how together they seem) and you never know what really goes on in other people's lives, so spend your energy improving on your own.

WILL THIS TAKE A LONG TIME?

Time—we never seem to have enough of it. Of course, if you had more time, you would have fixed this—and all your other issues—long ago, right? Most people have access to the tools they need to fix every area of their lives. But you keep waiting for something outside of you to change before you're willing to notice.

If you are pursuing happiness, it's time to consider if this is your biggest excuse. Time might not be a significant factor when your motivation is big enough.

The nastiest example of this is your health. You can say how important good nutrition and regular exercise are to your overall health, but do you take the time you feel you should in these areas to bring about change and experience happiness? Do you even take half an hour a day to exercise? But, when presented with a cancer diagnosis, an injury, or other health crisis, suddenly there is time. Suddenly, you can make time for the required physical therapy, exercise, doctor's visits, and treatments.

You see it as critical in those situations: you have to do it. You're focused on this area, and the motivation is limitless because it is suddenly about life or death.

You don't want to get to this point, but your reason for changing must be this important. Your willingness to do the work needs to be about life or death, because "Happiness Practices" are about precisely that: surviving or thriving. This is the purpose of the "Continuum Tool"—to reflect on the best- and worst-case scenarios in each area of your life. It's this awareness and the accompanying emotions that will serve as your motivation to do the work.

The internal reflection in each chapter will reveal what lies beneath the surface of your conscious mind. How much time will it take? It will take whatever time you choose to give it. Every person moves at their own pace. The more involved you are, the more critical your reason is, the more micro-actions you are willing to take, and the more progress you will see. The greater your involvement, the more significant the progress. The more significant the progress, the more possible the happiness will be.

Just start. Face the fear and try.

THE SEVEN HAPPINESS PRACTICES

INWARD REFLECTION

Where are you now? This question asks you to conduct a realistic appraisal of the landscape of your life. What is your current focus? And what is your intuition leading you to do? Are these aligned?

Once you focus correctly, you can direct your energy to match your true intentions. Knowing and acting in alignment will bring you to a place of authenticity and satisfaction that opens the space for greater happiness.

Inward reflection involves looking within yourself and examining your thoughts, feelings, and motivations. This self-awareness lets you understand your true desires, fears, and values. By gaining insight into your inner world, you can make more authentic choices, align your actions with your truth, and cultivate peace and contentment.

While turning your efforts to inward reflection, consider these questions. What happiness have you lost because you've made your happiness dependent on others, your income, your weight, or anything else you have limited control over?

It can be uncomfortable to face your inner thoughts and feelings. What shame are you hiding? You might uncover painful memories or truths about yourself. What guilt are you carrying?

Inward reflection is the source of emotional healing and personal growth, paving the way for a more authentic and fulfilling life.

THE POWER OF LANGUAGE

Words can shape your reality and influence your feelings and beliefs. They do not exist in isolation—every word you say aloud attaches itself to a story for the person who hears it.

Reflect on which words have the most power over you. What emotions are associated with these words in your story? Why? How often does the voice inside your head sound like this story? What if you could choose the sound of the voice, the words, and the intonation? What story would these new words tell? Imagine how that could change your experience. Imagine how words chosen intentionally and spoken with love could impact your happiness pulse.

Choosing words that convey hope, love, and encouragement can create a more positive and supportive environment for yourself and others. Affirmations and positive self-talk can rewire your brain, boost self-esteem, foster a positive outlook on life, and contribute to your happiness cadence.

EMOTIONS

Emotions are a fundamental aspect of the human experience. Understanding and managing your emotions is crucial for "Happiness Practices." By acknowledging and expressing your emotions in healthy ways, you can prevent them from becoming overwhelming or destructive and gain deeper insight into yourself. Learn to recognize what emotions you bring to an experience and how these shape your behavior. This is called emotional intelligence—being aware of and sensitive to your and others' emotions.

Emotional intelligence enhances your relationships and helps you navigate life's challenges more effectively by understanding how and why you appear. Emotions go hand in hand with inward reflection, so once you know what experiences have shaped your feelings, you will understand what emotions you are experiencing the world through.

This will allow you to start reframing these experiences and shifting their associated emotions.

EXPERIENCE AND ASSUMPTION AWARENESS

Your childhood, relationships with caregivers, culture, and education all shape your experiences and assumptions. By becoming aware of how your history influences your present reactions and the story you are telling yourself about your life, you can start to empower yourself by validating your experiences and any trauma that has led to your limiting beliefs.

This allows you to start reframing traumatic and negative experiences and see how adaptable and resilient you are. No matter what you have lived through, you are still here. That is power. This awareness allows you to break free from patterns that hinder your happiness and adopt a more compassionate and open-minded perspective to the narrative that drives your assumptions and emotions.

Your trauma is real. Your brain has a negativity bias, meaning it is more sensitive to negative experiences than positive ones. This bias helps you learn from and avoid pain, but it also makes painful memories more salient. These perceptions are the lens through which you currently see the world and are at the root of your painful emotions.

Validating this pain but acknowledging that you can do nothing to change what has already happened is the start of healing. Start practicing challenging your assumptions, reframing your experiences, and shifting your perceptions to see life as it is. This will free you from expectations that lead to disappointment and dissatisfaction.

FOCUS

You will attract and amplify these elements by focusing on the positive aspects of life, such as good nutrition, supportive friends, loving family, and overall health. Practicing gratitude and mindfulness helps shift your focus from problems to possibilities, enhancing your well-being.

What you choose to focus on grows stronger in your awareness, leading to a more optimistic and happy life. Distractions and multitasking can dilute focus and productivity. They can be a sign that you are avoiding uncomfortable emotions by doing internal reflection and keeping yourself busy on the surface, delaying having to look within.

Confirmation bias—looking for evidence to confirm what you already believe—can work against you. If you focus on finding evidence that life is difficult and that you always fail, this will become a self-fulfilling prophecy and perpetuate your suffering. However, confirmation bias can work for you if you can consciously harness it to reinforce positive beliefs and behaviors.

Focus can be reframed to what you search for, interpret, and remember. From this perspective, you can practice searching for, analyzing, and remembering everything in your life for which you are grateful, evidence of your success, and all the creativity you have cultivated in making a life for yourself. This is how you practice happiness.

THE MAGIC IN BEING PRESENT

Being present means fully engaging with the current moment without distraction or judgment. When you are present, you connect more deeply with yourself and others, savoring each moment as it comes. The magic of presence lies in its ability to make ordinary moments extraordinary, allowing you to notice your surroundings and have a whole sensory experience as the energy of life flows from you and through you.

The mind often wanders to past regrets or future worries. This is called rumination, and it is an evolutionary human behavior. Our ancestors needed to learn from negative experiences to survive, so remembering and analyzing threats and pain helped them to avoid these situations in the future. It is an attempt to problem-solve, but it is misplaced and only leads to further distress, widening the gap between you and happiness.

Presence reduces anxiety and stress by shifting focus away from past and future concerns and focusing on what you can control at the moment you're in. Being present allows you to fully experience the beauty around you and amplify gratitude, enhancing appreciation of life's moments and contributing to a more prosperous, more fulfilling life.

MICRO-ACTIONS

Small, consistent, intentional actions stacked together can lead to significant changes over time.

Life is made up of micro-actions that, when combined, tell a bigger story. Part of this work is to look at your objectives for each area of your life and say, *This is where I'd like to be,* and then break that objective down into micro-actions that can be achieved on a daily basis. You may ultimately achieve what initially seemed impossible. Celebrating micro-actions reinforces positive behavior and builds momentum.

Happiness must be practiced through ongoing micro-actions because change is inherently challenging, so people often give up before they even start and fail to achieve their goals. Recognizing and celebrating incremental progress makes the journey more sustainable and increases your likelihood of repeating them. Even if it seems unimportant or unimpactful, the sense of satisfaction in achievement will allow you to experience the happiness you are seeking.

Each "Happiness Practice" reinforces the others, and when stacked together over time, you will create a more aware and fulfilling life. Happiness is not a state to be achieved; it is the result of intentional actions taken to cultivate a radically different life than your current one. Happiness must be practiced, rumbled with, worked out, and ultimately chosen. Each chapter in Part Two of this book will teach you how to use the relevant "Happiness Practices" and associated micro-actions to take personal responsibility for your happiness.

Persistence is key on this journey because the path to happiness is often at odds with your comfort. You will need to overcome setbacks along the way, but the tools are simple, and if you are willing to do the work, what comes next is limitless.

PART
TWO

NUTRITION

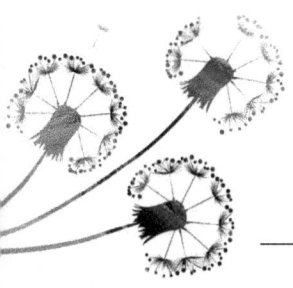

Our body is the only one we've been given,
so we need to maintain it;
we need to give it the best nutrition.
—TRUDIE STYLER

Before diving into your work in nutrition, remember to start with the "Continuum Tool" to help you reflect on what you are moving away from and toward in this area. The scenarios that you generate using this tool will help you connect with the emotions associated with each situation. These emotions become the motivation needed to propel you away from the pain of the worst-case situation and toward the pleasure of the best-case situation to reprioritize nutrition in your life. It is through these intentional micro-actions that you cultivate greater happiness.

By getting a better idea of the best- and worst-case scenarios, you will also be able to outline your goal for nutrition. Determining what this goal is will be your first micro-action. You can then use this larger goal to help you create smaller, more manageable micro-actions that can be incorporated into your life with far more ease. Remember to refer to "The Importance of Goals and Creating a Plan" in Part One for creating a plan for success, and

remember to download the "Goals," "Scheduling," and "Habits" resources from *nancysfreetools.com* to dive more deeply. Through these intentional micro-actions, you will build momentum and create a life that brings you happiness.

NUTRITIONAL CONTENT

Happiness is a dynamic state that results from conscious, continuous effort. There's a connection between what you eat, how your body processes food, and your overall happiness. A holistic approach to nutrition and metabolism provides a robust foundation for improving happiness through micro-actions.

People go to great lengths to take care of their pets and to make choices that are good for them. Parents spend time, money, and energy doing what is best for their children. So why do most people have such difficulty taking care of themselves?

Learning to love yourself, with all your imperfections and uniqueness, is a big part of finding internal peace and is a significant part of your journey to happiness. We are often tempted to compare ourselves to unrealistic images fed to us through the media and societal messaging. If you want to learn how to nourish yourself with food, you need to care enough about your body to want to show it kindness.

It is essential to consider the nutritional content of the food you consume. Every person has different dietary needs, so the first step to promoting your happiness through this area is to focus on what you eat, how these foods make you and your body feel, and what micro-actions you can take to improve your life in this area.

It's also a good idea to educate yourself about your body and its needs so that you can prevent diet-related issues rather than trying to reverse them.

For example, people lose muscle as they age; a reasonable protein intake can help mitigate that. If you realize this might be an issue, adding more protein to a few of your recipes is far simpler than correcting muscle wasting later.

ASSESS YOUR CURRENT STATE

The topic of nutrition, or as we have commonly come to think of nutrition and diet, is complex. Research is full of mixed messages and contradictory recommendations for food selection, and people have varying results.

The first step to any transformation is to assess your baseline. This means doing inward reflection to determine your current state. You must be honest with yourself at this stage and be as accurate as possible. This allows you to chart a healthy, safe, and realistic path.

In its simplest form, nutrition is relatively easy to manage. All the energy you consume can be measured in calories. You can then break the sources of these calories down into macronutrients. Macronutrients are the big-picture ingredients you are likely aware of, such as fats, carbohydrates, and proteins.

Micronutrients are also essential. These are all the different vitamins and minerals necessary for various bodily functions. Suppose you want to understand more about macro- and micronutrients and their impact on your body. In that case, there are countless resources available in books and online, but learning from a registered dietitian or nutritionist is a great place to start.

Some health clubs often have consultations available for anyone interested. And many health-insurance plans offer nutritional advice as part of their wellness offerings. If you want to do some reading on your own, I suggest you look for books focusing on understanding ingredients more than promoting a particular diet.

The most challenging part of tracking your calories is being honest about how much you consume and getting an accurate baseline to work with. The second most difficult part is being open to understanding why or analyzing your motivation for eating. Indeed, food is sustenance, but your food choices may be based entirely on other reasons.

As you become more honest about your consumption, soul search why you consume particular foods. Nutrition is an important aspect of your overall health and happiness, but sometimes there may be other aspects of your life that you need to address first. You may even need professional support.

But do not worry; once you have addressed those issues, you can always return to nutrition. Remember, micro-actions stack. This isn't a sprint; it's a marathon.

REFLECT AND DOCUMENT

The first step is to record whatever measurements you want to improve on; weight is standard. Then, reflect on what you consumed in the last seven days. If that's not possible at this time, start recording today. Document what you consumed, when, and the approximate quantity. If there is an emotional connection or rationalization for consuming it, record that too: special occasions, watching TV, breakfast, etc.

Now, start keeping a journal of what you eat during the upcoming week. Try to include the reasons why you ate. This can be an overwhelming task, but many tools can help you record your intake electronically, or feel free to record it in your journal.

The point of this step is to record and identify where your focus is. With this information, you can take your inward reflection to a slightly different level, where you can think about your eating patterns. The idea isn't to change any behavior or implement any micro-actions. Right now, you are only documenting your current behavior.

Most people skip this step because documenting isn't glamorous or comfortable. So, do you have to do it? The answer is yes. If you don't have an objective picture of where you are right now, you won't be able to take any significant micro-actions toward making realistic changes.

DOCUMENTATION AND RESOURCES

At this point, you should have two weeks of data: one from memory, even if it's just an estimation, and one recorded during the previous week as you have lived it. Now that you know what you consume and the times and frequency you consume it, you have the information you need to evaluate your choices and can determine what you want to adjust going forward.

You might initially be focused on metrics like your weight, but it is essential to look deeper and assess the micronutrients in your food, as well as anything else related to your health needs.

There are many reliable resources that can assist you in understanding calories, nutrients, micronutrients, and metabolism in more detail. Here are a few I find useful:

- *www.nutrition.gov* This is a USDA-sponsored website with basic dietary information.

- *www.hsph.harvard.edu/nutritionsource* This website is sponsored by Harvard University's Department of Public Health and provides a good collection of nutritional tips.

I also recommend content by Dr. Mark Hyman. His work provides an excellent resource for learning about nutrition and the way we metabolize foods.

Start with a simple plan for healthy eating, and don't fall into the trap of investing in a trend. Most diet and nutrition bestsellers fall into the trend category, so be careful.

MICRO-ACTIONS

You cannot break all of your bad habits overnight. Trying to do so will only set you up for failure and unhappiness. So, you must start by choosing one micro-action you can accomplish today.

It is often easier to start with something that you add to your daily routine rather than trying not to do something. For example, your first micro-action could be to improve your hydration by drinking more water during the day. Try drinking an eight-ounce glass of water before each meal.

Micro-actions allow you to reset your habits. From now on, every glass of water you drink must be celebrated and recognized as a victory. You are taking steps to change your life, which deserves to be honored.

Now, try to implement this micro-action for one week. Record your feelings about the micro-action and notice how it makes you feel. Celebrate yourself for taking this step and giving yourself a pat on the back every time. This is how you make the new behavior permanent. This is how you validate yourself as the resilient and powerful being you are!

EXERCISE

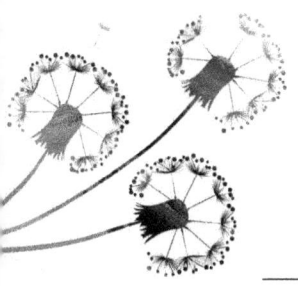

Exercise to stimulate, not annihilate.
The world wasn't formed in a day,
and neither were we.
Set small goals and build upon them.
— LEE HANEY

Before diving into exercise, remember to start with the "Continuum Tool" to help you reflect on what you are moving away from and toward in this area. The scenarios that you generate using the tool will help you connect with the emotions associated with each situation. These emotions become the motivation needed to propel you away from the pain of the worst-case situation and toward the pleasure of the best-case situation to reprioritize exercise in your life. It is through these intentional micro-actions that you cultivate greater happiness.

By getting a better idea of the best- and worst-case scenarios, you will also be able to outline your goal for exercise. Determining what this goal is will be your first micro-action. You can then use this larger goal to help you create smaller, more manageable micro-actions that can be incorporated into your life with far more ease. Remember to refer to "The Importance of Goals and Creating a Plan" in Part One for creating a plan for success, and

remember to download the "Goals," "Scheduling," and "Habits" resources from *nancysfreetools.com* to dive more deeply. Through these intentional micro-actions, you will build momentum and create a life that brings you happiness.

CREATING A REALISTIC ROUTINE

In high school, I wanted to be part of everything happening. I never tracked my steps, but between sports, running to classes, and work, I easily got 10,000 each day. My lifestyle was all about being active. I didn't have to think about it. But then college happened, and later work. I never quite felt as though I ever reached the point of the kind of regular movement I had achieved during my school days.

As I grew older, my lifestyle didn't feel healthy, and I didn't feel like I was exercising at all. So, I got a dog! I made time to do something different. I took him for a walk twice daily and usually made time for a hike with him on the weekend. It was busy, but it worked for me.

My focus wasn't on losing weight or changing my shape; it was feeling better. The simple action of getting a dog mushroomed into other micro-actions, like walking twice a day and going for hikes, which helped me create more direction in this area of my life. Instead of waiting for things to change in my work life, the "balance" illusion, I intentionally tried to bring happiness into my life.

The "Happiness Practices" aren't about waiting for everything outside of you to change—they're about doing the next right thing.

You have likely heard plenty of discussions about exercise. There are countless resources describing what you should do, how you should do it, and how often. But aim not to overcomplicate this area—simplify your next micro-action so that you can just *start*. Intentionally.

Remember, what you focus on will increase, so if you focus on all the ways you can't achieve happiness in this area (such as a busy schedule or finances), these beliefs will increase—along with your excuses! If you focus on how increased movement will make you happier, you will shift your priorities and find micro-actions to introduce into your life.

This shouldn't be too tricky to figure out, but be specific. Record what you have done during the previous week. Look at the week ahead, anticipate what you will be doing, and then track your activity as you go through the upcoming week. Measure everything. Look at the distance you walk, even if it is only around the house doing chores.

If you don't have a smartwatch to do this for you, get a pedometer and measure the distance you cover. Many apps, such as MyFitnessPal, can do this for you.

The focus here is a movement measurement, so do your best to document this accurately. If you do nothing, then document that. However, you can usually come up with some description of the activities you do, even if it's just how many times you go up and down the stairs. Doing nothing means you only sit at your desk or on the sofa or lie in bed all day. As a busy adult, it's unlikely you are truly inactive.

Once your documentation is done, the next step is to document where you are on the path and where you want to go. Use both the "Wheel of Life" and the "Continuum Tool" to help you.

In terms of exercise, there are two ends of the continuum. At one end is the genuine loafer: the person who rolls out of bed, has breakfast in front of the television, and only moves from that spot to get more food. That would be a good representation of no movement at all. At the other end of the scale, you might see professional or Olympic athletes who live to train and only stop the movement long enough to re-energize their bodies. Somewhere in the middle fall the rest of us.

Every person has a different view of the ideal amount of movement and a distinct image of what perfect body that movement should produce. You must accurately measure where you are on this continuum and then clearly set your objective.

Be careful! This section is not about your weight but about developing an awareness of your movement and understanding how you can shift your focus to health over shape. Weight loss may be a byproduct of increased movement, but remember: true happiness is experienced not through a state of external change but internal shifts. Realize, for example, that your body is not responsible for your unhappiness; rather, your beliefs about certain bodies being unacceptable leads you to treat yourself with a lack of love, and, as such, experience an absence of peace with yourself, a core component of happiness.

Your success in this area means working toward feeling happier by being present with your body as it moves, practicing gratitude for all the ways your body can move and serve you, and developing the micro-actions that enhance your awareness of the power of your body and the magic of being in the present moment and not focused on whether your body is changing or not.

Happiness in this area is not measured in inches—it is measured in the moments you realize you are alive, breathing, and strong.

START SMALL AND KEEP IT EASY

It's up to you to determine what goal you would like to achieve. Being honest about where your focus lies, resetting that focus, and applying the micro-actions will get you to your desired location.

As you think about your goals in this area, remember the well-supported concept that every person should move their body for at least thirty minutes daily. This minimum activity may be achievable for some, and for others, it will be a goal to work toward.

Moving your body enough will help you experience happiness by boosting the feel-good hormones (dopamine, serotonin, endorphins, and oxytocin) your body naturally produces during exercise. Regular movement means regular hormones—you choose to pursue happiness actively!

If the movement you decide to engage in is something you enjoy and can do repeatedly, you'll be more likely to make it a regular part of your life. This activity should increase your heart rate above its resting rate. You don't need to be exhausted at the end of thirty minutes, but you should feel that you have worked your muscles.

Reflect on a time when you were more physically active than you currently are. What were the activities that you participated in at that time? Many people can return to a high school experience such as a team sport involving regular practices. It could be a basketball team, track team, or swim team. When the season ended or you left the sport or graduated, the regular movement that came with it likely changed. Maybe you never replaced it.

Now, try to remember what you enjoyed about that activity. What was it that kept you doing it? Would it be possible to get some of that excitement back again? Would there be a way for you to restart that activity or something similar?

Spend some time reflecting inward and seeing what was appealing about movement in the past and what you could revive. This is your first micro-action in this area: determining which activity you enjoyed most.

Start small if you have never been physically active and want to start now. One of the easiest activities to start is walking or taking the stairs. Both are perfect micro-actions to start your movement journey and can easily be done progressively and with increasing intensity.

A short ten-minute walk down your street can be increased to a walk to the next block, and so on. Listen to your favorite podcast or audiobook while you walk, and you might even be tempted to keep walking to hear the next chapter! And don't forget to celebrate every small victory, even if you only made it to the end of your street!

Once you have started implementing a simple micro-action like a walking routine into your life, it's time for your next micro-action so you can start stacking them.

Far too many people set themselves up to fail and give up on their goals because they expect too much from themselves too soon. Change is difficult, so you must take it one small step at a time.

Your next micro-action involves looking a bit further and trying to find a different movement that might be fun and that you would likely repeat. The easiest activities to get involved in are ones that have social components. Sometimes, that could be adding a friend to your walking routine or joining a walking club. Other times, it might mean finding a partner for tennis, golf, or racquetball.

Swimming is an excellent sport to pick up later in life since it is easy for aging joints! The beauty of swimming is that you can do it at your own pace, and most major cities have public pools and swimming clubs.

There are also lots of good reasons to try something new. Suppose your next micro-action is signing up for a new activity. In that case, you will not have unrealistic expectations for yourself and may enjoy the novelty of the new activity, which can keep you interested for longer.

The list is infinite. Find something that is a fit for you and your life.

It's often said that you cannot expect it to become a habit until you do an activity successfully for at least twenty-one days. Whether or not twenty-one days is the exact figure, incorporating these micro-actions into your daily life for at least three weeks is how you stack micro-actions together to develop the discipline that will help you make consistent choices that lead to overall happiness.

The bottom line is this: Consistent micro-actions mean that it will start to get easier over time. And the more manageable the movement becomes, the more happiness you will gain.

WE ALL GET DERAILED

One of the biggest mistakes you can make when starting an exercise journey is biting off more than you can chew. Be honest with yourself, and don't take on too much. Do what you know you can maintain. And don't beat yourself up if you skip a day.

The next micro-action is simple. When the first micro-actions you have taken become a habit, slowly add activity or increase the time you spend doing the activity. This is particularly important regarding exercise.

It is easy to get overwhelmed or exhausted, or even injure yourself when starting something for the first time. The initial excitement will fade, and you may experience an emotional or mental slump.

So, if you are at the end of the continuum where you feel that you are doing minimal exercise or activity—maybe your activity is limited to folding and putting away the laundry—add a few additional flights of stairs to your routine during the day or walk between rooms a few times a day. If you already do thirty minutes of daily exercise, add a few more minutes to your current activity or add activity, like a sauna or some stretching.

Adding just an extra five or ten minutes per day adds a significant amount of time over a week.

If you find you cannot maintain the added activity, then you need to take a step back. Instead of adding ten minutes to your daily exercise routine, only add two minutes and work your way up.

It's not about how your body looks on the outside that will bring you happiness; it's about the person you are becoming every time you decide to do something for yourself and experience the feeling of satisfaction that comes with every single achievement.

ACCOUNTABILITY IS CRITICAL

The more accountable you can be for your micro-actions, the greater your chances of success. Feeling like you are part of a group or that someone expects you to be somewhere makes it more difficult for you to devise rational reasons for missing the exercise.

If you are not part of a group, the people closest to you may be the best people to ask assistance from, but don't discount the value of sharing this with your journal, a distant friend, or even a stranger!

Accountability is the next micro-action.

Remember, happiness is experienced when you intentionally shift your focus to abundance and not by ruminating on failure. The more often you say your intention out loud, the more likely it is to become a reality.

Consider choosing someone like the stranger at your daily coffee shop stop who asks you how you're doing.

Give them an update, like, "I'm here after my class again—that's twice this week!" They may not care at all, and it may seem like small talk to them, but this micro-action will help you empower yourself by admitting your victory out loud.

Being accountable also changes your perspective on the goal. Share your plans for changing your routine before you get started. This verbalization helps your subconscious normalize the change and plan for it. It may feel silly, but this will help you to get the emotional buy-in needed to follow through on the new goal.

If you are a novice at accountability and it makes you a bit nervous, you must find the micro-action with which you are comfortable. At the very least, you need to journal your intentions. Write down what you plan to do. In this way, you are at least accountable to yourself.

The journal is the place where you can rationalize why you did not meet your goals, as well as the place to document all your excuses. Seeing them written down can help you identify why you keep making them! You won't be able to experience the fruits of the "Happiness Practices" if you keep looking for shortcuts.

If you need more stringent accountability in this area beyond what you can do for yourself, consider finding a coach.

Until you have made the activity a habit, you need some of this accountability to keep you on track. Just remember, you made the conscious decision to do the new activity. It was your choice, and no one is forcing you. You have control over your life, and you are responsible for your behaviors. Happiness must be worked for, and you must do the work.

PERSONAL TIME

*Even though you're growing up,
you should never stop having fun.*
— Nina Dobrev

Before diving into your personal time, remember to start with the "Continuum Tool" to help you reflect on what you are moving away from and toward in this area. The scenarios that you generate using the tool will help you connect with the emotions associated with each situation. These emotions become the motivation needed to propel you away from the pain of the worst-case situation and toward the pleasure of the best-case situation to reprioritize personal time in your life. It is through these intentional micro-actions that you cultivate greater happiness.

By getting a better idea of the best- and worst-case scenarios, you will also be able to outline your goal for personal time. Determining what this goal is will be your first micro-action. You can then use this larger goal to help you create smaller, more manageable micro-actions that can be incorporated into your life with far more ease. Remember to refer to "The Importance of Goals and Creating a Plan" in Part One for creating a plan for success, and

remember to download the "Goals," "Scheduling," and "Habits" resources from *nancysfreetools.com* to dive more deeply. Through these intentional micro-actions, you will build momentum and create a life that brings you happiness.

HOW TO CARVE OUT TIME

Personal time should be a regular part of your life, even when you are filling your responsible adult shoes. Carving out a space in your life for personal time requires shifting your focus from others to yourself and implementing the necessary micro-actions to allow you to experience the magic of being present in your life.

There was a time in my life when I had no personal time. I lived in a new city, had two small children, and had no social life. I missed having fun, and I missed feeling happy. Life had become so predictable, and instead of finding ways to be curious about my new life and exploring the possibility of experiencing happiness in new ways, I was plodding through my life on autopilot. Once I realized that it was my responsibility to find the happiness I was longing for, I slowly started introducing micro-actions that gradually got me out of the house, allowing me to find ways to squeeze in some fun things.

When my first child was a few months old, my husband and I were invited to go skiing. We stayed in a hotel and got a babysitter who could call me if I was urgently needed. Sure enough, the phone rang. The call came in when I was at the top of the ski lift, and it took twenty minutes before I could rescue the babysitter from my screaming daughter.

In the moment, I felt selfish and guilty, but I never forgot the brief and wonderful feeling of being outdoors that day. I was present, *fully present,* to the beauty all around me. I felt happy.

You need to take care of yourself to be the best for others.

Personal time can be broken into a variety of different packages. Like everything else, your first micro-action is to start with your baseline. That way, you can discover where you are right now. Then you can decide where you want to go and how you will get there.

Determining your baseline starts with a retrospective analysis of the past week, remembering where you spent time, and then a prospective study of where you expect to spend time on yourself in the upcoming week. Finally, live through a week and document it as it happens.

These should be your fundamental micro-actions.

Ensure you are honest about your reflection to develop a realistic plan for incorporating micro-actions to increase personal time. The reflection and documentation may reveal things you would not otherwise have realized.

FILLING YOUR CUP

First, document everything you currently do for yourself and then everything you intend to do for yourself.

If right now you aren't achieving these, that's fine. These tasks will become your goals in this area.

Take note of the times of day that you usually find pockets of time for yourself. Give credit to anything that "fills up the cup"—every micro-action must be celebrated!

The filling of your cup involves anything that feels good, that you enjoy, and that, when completed, brings you a sense of satisfaction. These micro-actions make you feel alive and energized, aware of the magic of the present moment. They will be different for each person.

What fills up the cup for one may be exhausting for another. Document what makes you feel energized, not necessarily what is socially desirable in this area. Happiness requires authenticity in practice, being true to yourself and knowing what *you* need. Micro-actions taken because of another person's expectations of you will only lead to more disconnection and less satisfaction.

For example, one person may enjoy reading a magazine in the doctor's office because this might be the only time he or she gets to enjoy a magazine and be quiet, while another person may see this time as stressful and wasteful. Recognize the times that you feel fulfilled by the activity, no matter how small it seems.

Now, for those saying, "I take no time for myself. Everything I do is a required activity," take the time to do some internal reflection. Are you being honest with yourself? It is unlikely that there is not something you are doing for yourself, something that gives you some positive reinforcement or a reason to keep going back to it outside of purely having to do it.

These things might be difficult to identify if they are habitual.

Human beings are creatures of habit, but that habit is formed by reinforcement. So, if you struggle to identify and document the actions themselves, consider their outcomes. The positive reinforcement might be from others—even just hearing them say thank you—or the sense of satisfaction you feel after a job well done.

After some consideration, you should be able to document at least a few items you do for yourself each day. To support you in your reflection, download the "Self Analysis" document found in the Personal Time folder at *nancysfreetools.com*.

The temptation here is to continue reading. But seeing your life as it is right now is critical. You need to know where you are to see where you are going and figure out how to get there. Happiness cannot be achieved until you are ready to accept your life as it looks at this moment—the good and the bad. Stop, reflect, and take some time to journal your thoughts.

INNER CHILD

Is there a person in your life who brings out your inner child? Your inner child is the playful part of you, the part of yourself that you likely tucked away when you "grew up."

Some people may think being playful is childish, but that's the point! Young children worry less about what other people think and can be more authentic. They express themselves freely and are usually motivated by curiosity, so they are always willing to try new things.

Your inner child is the most creative part of yourself—and it will teach you how to be silly again! Sometimes, this inner child materializes to make everything beautiful and take an experience from the ordinary to the wonderful. This creates a sense of magic that takes any experience from routine to memorable.

Being childlike is about letting your guard down. This is a quality worth cultivating. It's about embedding yourself in the enchantment of your life, forgetting the restrictions of being a grown-up, and asking yourself what would be fun to do. It is not the same as being foolish; it is simply laughing for the sake of laughing and opening yourself up to the flow of your life, experiencing happiness in the moment. Other people who have learned this gift are usually the people who make you smile and remind you of what you believed was possible before the world told you it wasn't. Spending time with these people and observing how they approach their lives can provide you with valuable insight into how you can take life a little less seriously when it matters and find opportunities to have more fun.

Now that you have completed the documentation that reflects your personal time, it's a good time to add another micro-action to your routine. A childlike micro-action. Choose a micro-action that is indulgent or one that feels selfish! Children are usually very good at being greedy and caring for their needs. This doesn't have to be a bad thing!

For many, this will be challenging work. Implementing a micro-action that only serves you and your inner child will be difficult. For others, this may be easier. Some micro-actions you can start implementing in this area include writing in a diary, reading for pure pleasure, or meditating. It might be lying on the grass in your garden, looking at the clouds, going on a picnic, or doing some art. It might even be cranking your favorite song and taking a dance break.

Consider taking some time to put a journaling micro-action into practice here. Write down which other micro-actions that connect you with your inner child you would like to introduce into your life and how they make you feel. This work doesn't need to produce an immediate change; it is designed to raise awareness at this stage. When last did you allow yourself to be silly? When last did you laugh out loud? When last did you color with crayons or make something out of clay? Use your imagination to connect with your inner child and indulge your imagination!

For many people, this is uncharted territory. Most of us neglect the things that we wholeheartedly enjoy in favor of taking care of everyone else. So, consider what you haven't done for years, and add this to your micro-action list. To foster happiness, you need to recognize what you are not doing for yourself.

If you aren't sure what to do, spend some time observing children, and then mimic what you see them do! It could be as simple as doing a cartwheel, swinging at the park, or even treating yourself to an ice-cream cone on a hot summer day.

A FULL CUP

Understanding the feelings associated with a "full cup" is crucial. Knowing that these micro-actions make you feel happy, satisfied, connected, hopeful, and alive, you will understand why emotions are important. It's not about waiting for the happy feeling to rise in you; it's about the micro-actions that you intentionally incorporate into your life that bring the happy feelings to you.

Finding ways to recognize when your cup is full and what micro-actions create this feeling is key.

One of the biggest stumbling blocks in the pursuit of happiness is the feeling that you do not deserve it. During childhood, you form beliefs about people and the world based on what happens around you—good and bad. These experiences may affect your self-esteem as an adult who operates within these invisible frameworks. For example, if someone you trusted told you you weren't good enough, you may see life through the lens of this flawed belief, telling yourself that you're an unworthy person. If you feel like you are not worthy of happiness, you may build a life that reflects this—including sabotaging opportunities that could lead to happiness.

Starting to believe that you are worthy of happiness means starting to unravel decades of conditioning, untangling the limiting beliefs that have been attached to your identity. You are worthy of happiness; to experience it, you must learn to support yourself through this stage of your awakening. It all starts with a single micro-action: being brave enough to try.

One of the fantastic things about building strong social connections in your life is the support you build. Recognize that social connections are a key tenet of fostering happiness in your life—not just for the pleasure of sharing another person's life story but also for carrying you when you need support.

Every human being is worthy of personal time. So much of this work is individual work, but recognize the power of asking for help when you need it. You don't have to carry more on your own; you need to make an intentional decision to allow yourself to be vulnerable. This could mean being vulnerable about why you find it difficult to give yourself personal time. With your social network's support, you can reach your goals more easily than you ever will on your own.

So what does "fill your cup" and "find fun" mean? Let's dig a bit deeper.

Travel back to a time in your life when you planned everything around what was happening on the weekend and how much you could fit into those few days. I'm sure you were young and full of energy! Did you experience happiness? Over time, your desire to use that same energy has likely changed. Introducing fun micro-actions daily, weekly, monthly, and annually is a good objective to bring some of this intentionality back into your life.

This can be as simple as the attitude you bring to your day, creating a mood of celebration and a sense of playfulness by getting excited. Having something fun to look forward to is also a great way to increase motivation and shift your focus when feeling glum.

Things are more fun when shared with others, so try to add other people to your plans for fun. Starting with micro-actions is once again key. What can you do each day that will make you feel happy? Daily activities include watching funny YouTube videos or a tickle fight with your partner or kids. Weekly fun might consist of entertainment or participating in socially engaging sports.

In addition to all these micro-actions, planning vacations away from home can be great fun—anything from one night away in a nearby Airbnb to international travel counts. Even the micro-action of planning the trip can be as much fun as the event itself! It can even be as simple as celebrating your routine and toasting an ordinary family supper with sparkling juice, candles, dressing up, or indulging in more than one dessert.

It's important to note there is value in creating a beautiful environment that enhances the senses. Your sensory experiences drive your perceptions and emotions. Some of these sensory experiences can be intentionally brought into your everyday routines. Consider music, like hearing a particular song or tune and being "transported in time" to an earlier experience in your life. Consider playing music in your environment, even if it's just you alone at home folding the laundry, and see how this affects your feelings. This same micro-action can be taken with all your senses, like baking your favorite cookies and enjoying the aroma that wafts through the house.

Try burning scented candles or incense periodically to change the scent of your space. Buy flowers, and rather than having a single vase, separate them and place them in various places to enjoy them on a larger scale—your bedroom, workspace, and kitchen. These small touches bring beauty and enhance your quality of life.

MENTAL STRENGTH

There will always be obstacles and challenges that stand in your way. Building mental strength will help you develop resilience to those potential hazards so you can continue on your journey to success.

— AMY MORIN

Before diving into your mental strength, remember to start with the "Continuum Tool" to help you reflect on what you are moving away from and toward in this area. The scenarios that you generate using the tool will help you connect with the emotions associated with each situation. These emotions become the motivation needed to propel you away from the pain of the worst-case situation and toward the pleasure of the best-case situation to reprioritize how you can improve your mental strength. It is through these intentional micro-actions that you cultivate greater happiness.

By getting a better idea of the best- and worst-case scenarios, you will also be able to outline your goal for mental strength. Determining what this goal is will be your first micro-action. You can then use this larger goal to help you create smaller, more manageable micro-actions that can be incorporated into your life with far more ease. Remember to refer to "The Importance of Goals and Creating a Plan" in Part One for creating a plan

for success, and remember to download the "Goals," "Scheduling," and "Habits" resources from *nancysfreetools.com* to dive more deeply. Through these intentional micro-actions, you will build momentum and create a life that brings you happiness.

WHY FIND PURPOSE?

So, what exactly do we mean when we talk about mental strength? Mental strength is the ability to manage and master negative thoughts, uncomfortable emotions, and challenging circumstances. It is a measure of perseverance through obstacles to achieve your goals. Mental strength is characterized by self-discipline, adaptability, and focus—especially in the face of trials.

Having a clear sense of purpose provides a strong foundation for mental strength. Keeping your eye on the bigger picture and your overall dreams and goals allows you to find direction when you lose your way and keeps you from giving up when things get complicated. Purpose fuels resilience— the power to get up after you fail and try again. If you know where you want to go, you will always find a way.

Purpose stimulates mental strength because it gives your suffering meaning—it gives you a reason to endure difficult times.

Do you know your purpose? Finding the answer to this question can be your life's true source of happiness, the driving force that keeps you motivated to leave your mark on the world.

Finding purpose in life is not something most young people think about. High school and college graduates are typically focused on finding a job where they will earn enough income to cover their monthly expenses. But reflecting back on this time in your own life might provide you with some insight into what you were passionate about when you were young and very few things seemed out of your reach!

So, rather than starting where you are right now, turn back time a little bit. Reflect on when this question was asked of you the first time: "What do you want to be when you grow up?" Use this memory or a similar memory to turn your mind to a vision you once had of your purpose or mission. What was it about the lifestyle or profession that you respected or wanted to emulate as a child or young adult? What characteristics attracted you and allowed you to believe, even naïvely, that you could be just like them? What story did you want your life to tell?

Deep within us all is a desire to leave a legacy, to make the world a better place.

Maybe you outgrew the desires of your inner child; maybe your passions changed, or you chose the safe option. Whatever led you to where you are now, it's essential to understand that mental strength is the ability to adapt, change, and grow. This does not mean it's too late to nurture your purpose now. You have developed your character and worn different hats over the years—you are more equipped than ever to discover your purpose.

When exploring your purpose, remember to reflect on the life you have already lived. It has not been for nothing. My purpose has gone from wanting to be a dolphin trainer as a child to being a photographer, nurse, mother, and educator. Your purpose can and will change as you grow, so be open to your focus shifting.

Be mindful of the language you use to describe your life. Have you been a full-time parent for decades and describe this time as a waste? Did you choose a career that would provide for your family, but it meant you had to sacrifice your passion? What words do you use to describe these years of your life or yourself now? Can you shift your focus to see how you have grown because of these years and choose words that make you feel empowered, proud, and happy?

The following section will help you reframe the narrative of your life and assist you in determining your purpose using the power of language and micro-actions.

THE POWER OF LANGUAGE
WHEN DISCOVERING YOUR PURPOSE

Reflecting on those moments from your youth when you felt passionate about something can help remind you of what drives you. Try to remember your youthful attitude. What was important to you? What made you believe that anything was possible? What kinds of words did you use to talk about these passions, and how did these words make you feel?

The first micro-action for rediscovering your purpose will help you recall what may have made you feel zealous. Passion in the pursuit of a dream or goal will enhance your experience of happiness in every area of your life. Remember a few youthful visions of "what I want to be when I grow up." Take the time to reflect on your memories of those you respected and looked up to, and think of the qualities you saw in them that allowed you to relate or connect to them. Maybe it was a grandparent that was very special. Perhaps it was a visitor to your home or a leader in your community. Think of the qualities that you were drawn to, and document the characteristics that come to mind.

Now, consider the words you chose to describe this person. What emotions do these words make you feel? How do these emotions differ from those you feel when you tell the story of your life as it is now? Can you feel the energy difference between these choices of words? Remember—words carry powerful emotive messages. They impact the way you see yourself and your experiences.

The next micro-action toward mental strength is to reflect on one of your first job experiences. My first paid job was as a swimming teacher. It helped me to gain confidence and feel more comfortable expressing myself in front of people. The choice of these words, "confident," "assertive," and "respected," make me feel powerful and capable. I look at that time as a great stepping stone for my future in nursing, where I had to make rapid decisions under high stress, and having the confidence to trust my decisions was key.

In contrast, had I focused on words like "social anxiety" when I had to talk to crowds, or "insecurity" because I was unsure about being responsible for children, I would have developed a narrative of inadequacy.

Most people had job experiences in high school or through college that were part-time and unrelated to their career of choice later on. If this is you, think about what got you into those positions. Why did you end up taking those jobs? Were you out searching for the job or did you create it for yourself? What was it about those first few jobs that appealed to you, or what were you skilled at? Think about the words used to describe you during this time. Write those words down somewhere you can see them.

What motivated you to be productive in this or any other work that came after, and what did you find fun about them? Writing down the answers to these questions will help you unlock areas of passion, label your language, and identify what your self-talk sounds like.

Self-criticism erodes self-esteem, increasing the likelihood that you will doubt your abilities and anticipate failure, weakening your mental strength and compromising the possibility of you discovering your passions and pursuing your purpose. Conversely, self-affirmation and encouragement, which are practiced with your self-talk, boost your self-esteem and generate the kind of energy you need to persevere and fight for the life you want. So remember, keep your writing honest.

HOW DOES THIS AFFECT ME NOW?

Let's fast forward to your current life. The next micro-action is looking more deeply into your strengths and reflecting on your skills.

Most people have had more than one career or more than one job. Even if you have been doing the same job for years, the job itself has probably changed. Your experiences around those jobs will have changed, too, along with how you describe them. Where once you were excited and optimistic, you may find that you now complain and feel resentful.

Reflect on how you view your current job. Then, reflect on how you get paid to do your current job. If you don't have recent paid-work experience, consider your most recent volunteer work experience. Or, if it is full-time care of your children, consider the cost of replacing what you do and the variety of skills it would take to replace you.

It's not critical to have an incredibly accurate hourly rate. The idea is to get an estimation of the dollar value of your work. Note the skill set that allows you to be in that position. Even if it seems insignificant, write something down, even if the only thing that qualified you for the position is that you said yes.

Now look at what you have to do to keep that job. Understanding your value is not just monetary. You bring unique skills to everything you do. Recognizing this value and knowing how to maintain it is vital for self-discovery. Instead of focusing on the aspects of the job you don't like, focus on all the skills you bring to the job. This will help you shift the language you use when describing it and help you find greater purpose in it.

You are a powerful, talented human being who brings something to the table whenever you show up.

Any workplace demands that you continually try to improve yourself. Rather than competing with your colleagues, intentionally trying to be happy and finding purpose means only trying to be better than the person you were yesterday. Unquestioningly, joining the rat race will not bring you to a life of authenticity and happiness; understanding the mental strength you have to overcome, learn, adapt, and grow is how you start to see yourself as you are—dynamic, formidable, and passionate!

Armed with this knowledge, now consider what you want to learn next.

Continued education is a vital skill for purpose and happiness. Any job, career, or purpose requires knowledgeable, experienced individuals willing to work hard. Raising enough motivation to learn a new skill will help you raise enough motivation to work for your happiness. What you do in one area of your life affects all areas.

Learning keeps you alive and relevant. Perhaps happiness eludes you because you assume that one day, happiness will be automatic if you get the "right" degree and the "right" job, marry the "right" person, and live in the "right" neighborhood. Have you been waiting to stop working so hard?

You can't stop.

Happiness is not terminal; it's a continuous state of learning, growing, and rediscovering your purpose while rediscovering your true self.

The good news is that you don't need to keep learning in one particular area. If you are a trained professional in almost any area, you have been learning your whole life and will likely continue increasing your knowledge.

That is not what you need to do. Instead, keep your mind awake and alert. You could learn about planting tomatoes, how your child's school board functions, car maintenance, or how to speak a new language. Think about the areas of your life that have interested you and what made you feel excited and passionate.

Refresh your memory about subjects or topics you have previously learned about, especially those you have genuinely enjoyed learning. Find something you want to learn more about. Reflect on your younger self and the skills you have remembered you possess. What did you focus on learning back then? What do you want to learn more about now?

FUTURE LEARNING

You want to reawaken that vision for learning because, without an active mind and the desire to continue to learn, you can become complacent, which can lead to complacency in other areas of life, including your pursuit of happiness. Complacency wears down your mental health, your physical health, and your overall well-being.

One of the biggest excuses I hear for not continuing to learn new things is, "I don't have time." The truth is, human beings always manage to find the time to do the things they think are important enough. If it's truly something important to you or truly something you want to do, you make the time to do it. When the stakes are high enough, you find a way. You rearrange your life to make time for children, spouses, friends, or family. So if it's important enough to you, you can even rearrange your time for learning!

Instead of focusing on how you will make the time, focus on what you want to make time for. How would your life be different if you had this knowledge? Would you feel more aligned with your purpose or more qualified to ask for what you want? Would you feel happier?

The micro-action that matters here is shifting your focus to placing value on the new knowledge. For example, if you want to learn to speak Russian or Japanese, what is that going to do for you? Are you planning to travel to Japan? If you decide you want to learn how to do your own car maintenance, why do you want to learn more about cars? Is it because you don't trust your mechanic, or maybe because you've always wanted to buy an old sports car?

Think about the value of having this new knowledge. Once you start reframing your focus from *how* you will learn to *why* you want to learn, you discover where passion lies. When you feel that passion, you will direct your micro-actions accordingly.

THE WHY

Your next micro-action is to start to get clear on the details. Be creative. Consider: What words are you using to describe your new knowledge? How and why does this knowledge align with your purpose? How can this knowledge benefit you? Where will it take you? Explain to yourself why it is crucial to have this knowledge.

When crafting your narrative about why it's important for you to have this new knowledge, use words like "I can" and "I will." Changing your narrative to the "I can" and "I will" perspective will help your subconscious understand and find the reasons to move forward into the next micro-action.

At this point, your journal entries should reflect at least one area in which you would like to learn new knowledge, something you are interested in, and why. To help you dive deeply and gain more clarity regarding your why, use the "7 Levels Deep" tool found at *nancysfreetools.com*. This tool helps you to get past your superficial reasons for wanting something and into your deeper reasons for taking action. This clarity will propel you to take consistent action.

The next micro-action will help you figure out how you will find the time to acquire the new knowledge. Try a scheduling exercise, and mark any "unused time." This is where you start.

Plugging extra things into your already busy life is tough to do. However, with the value placed on learning, it will be easier to find the time. Remember, it is all about the micro-actions. It is not about changing your life overnight. You can seek and find happiness right here, right now, by the next micro-action you take. By choosing language that sparks creativity and solutions rather than fear and failure and shifting your focus to more knowledge, passion, and ability, you are giving yourself the power you need to experience happiness amid your ordinary life.

Constantly moving forward and continuously challenging yourself will keep your mind learning and will keep you aligned with the happiness you seek. You will know you have stopped learning when you stop feeling challenged. You will know you aren't being challenged when you feel too comfortable or even bored. When your micro-actions become routine, it's time to amp them up. Lean into and feel the challenge. Experience the happiness in the process of creating the life you have always dreamed of. That is your benchmark to know you are succeeding and growing.

Accountability, as always, is highly recommended. Find someone who can help you be accountable for the decisions you choose to make in this area, or journal using an electronic or paper journal. Whatever you choose, the important part is to update it regularly.

Find some routine to which you can tack onto the activity: maybe during your coffee break, or it might be easier to remember it at bedtime. The journaling micro-action in itself has value. So, even if you cannot learn something new right now, consider taking on the journaling micro-action. Writing rewires your neural pathways, which means you are growing, allowing you to observe the power of language in your life. Seeing the words you use to talk about yourself and your ability to learn and grow will motivate you to choose kinder words that will generate emotions of self-love and happiness.

SPIRITUAL HEALTH

More fundamental than religion is our basic human spirituality. We have a basic human disposition towards love, kindness and affection irrespective of whether we have a religious framework or not. When we nurture this most basic resource—when we set about cultivating those basic inner values which we all appreciate in others, then we start to live spiritually.

— DALAI LAMA

Before diving into your spiritual health, remember to start with the "Continuum Tool" to help you reflect on what you are moving away from and toward in this area. The scenarios that you generate using the tool will help you connect with the emotions associated with each situation. These emotions become the motivation needed to propel you away from the pain of the worst-case situation and toward the pleasure of the best-case situation to reprioritize your spiritual health. It is through these intentional micro-actions that you cultivate greater happiness.

By getting a better idea of the best- and worst-case scenarios, you will also be able to outline your goal for spiritual health. Determining what this goal is will be your first micro-action. You can then use this larger goal to help you create smaller, more manageable micro-actions that can be incorporated into your life with far more ease. Remember to refer to "The Importance of Goals and Creating a Plan" in Part One for creating a plan

for success, and remember to download the "Goals," "Scheduling," and "Habits" resources from *nancysfreetools.com* to dive more deeply. Through these intentional micro-actions, you will build momentum and create a life that brings you happiness.

START WHERE YOU ARE

Spirituality: what does it mean to you? Is it important? How do you feel about incorporating it into your daily life? In my experience, many people place a low priority on this in today's world, but it can be beneficial to include spirituality into your life—even if you aren't religious.

So, what is spiritual health and why should you care about it? Some people come from a background that supports being part of a religious community. Attending services regularly and learning the values of that culture were a big part of their experiences. However, that is much less common in many communities today.

Spiritual health can be an essential component of happiness. The traditional environment of structured religion provided families and individuals with focus—guidelines and frequent reminders about how to live as a good person, practice inward reflection, be present, and contemplate things far more significant than themselves. If you have no interest in finding a way to do this in a religious community, you can still benefit by looking for ways to do it in other spaces.

When you shift your focus inward and apply spirituality to self-improvement, you can experience more happiness and become a greater force in your communities and the world.

FINDING A TIME AND PLACE FOR SPIRITUALITY

Human beings are community creatures. We function best as members of a group, and we create more successfully when we share ideas.

Historically, we have relied on our families to build our communities, but over the last one hundred years, the importance of collectivism has decreased, particularly in Western cultures where individualism is emphasized.

Where social systems once offered the support we needed to grow, now technology has taken its place. Human beings have never been more connected but disconnected in the history of the world, thanks to the sometimes false sense of community it provides. We rely heavily on the metaverse to meet all our needs, but we still really need to be in the physical community of others, in a social space, and to feel the energy of people around us.

During COVID-19, the world became proficient at Zoom. However, those who could choose the in-person experiences almost universally reported that their contact was more impactful, meaningful, and fulfilling.

Finding people to connect with can come in the form of a religious community. Many religious groups are open and welcoming to members and nonmembers alike. Many groups are open to people dropping in and seeing if the community fits their needs.

Your first micro-action could be exploring your community. You will likely find several possible groups, some religious and others not explicitly so. You must feel the space is honest and accepting, aligned with your values, and offers valuable support.

Many people have become disillusioned with formal religious organizations, but many honest and supportive communities are out there. You may need to do some inward reflection here and challenge the assumptions you have about religious organizations before you are willing to explore your community.

Your life story may include spiritual disillusionment, and the damage of those experiences has led you to mistrust people of authority within religious spaces and sow seeds of doubt about anyone claiming to care about your spiritual health. This is a valid reality for many people, and I am not advocating for putting yourself in any discomfort. I want to acknowledge the immense strength it requires to even consider what your journey of spirituality looks like. It is yours and yours alone and does not need to fit anyone's expectations. My hope is that if you are a person who has been a victim of spiritual disillusionment and are still seeking spiritual sanctuary in a safe community, whenever you feel ready to do so, may you find a space that respects and honors the discomfort you have endured and allows you to define for yourself what your spiritual journey looks like. These communities exist, even if only to hold space for your grief.

If you are a person who currently feels like your spiritual life is lacking and this is having a significant effect on your happiness, you can take several steps to start shifting your focus away from discomfort of the past and toward the promise of the future. If you would like to explore your spirituality, and you feel ready to do so, ask yourself this: What did it feel like to be a part of something greater than yourself, to be present in the collective moment and experience the magic it held? Does this feel like happiness?

You can take part in other micro-actions besides a formal community to connect spiritually. The first micro-action is spending regular time reflecting on your life experiences, on what you learned today or this week—whether it's in the area of the new knowledge you have gained, from a conversation with someone new, or on something you have read.

The second micro-action that benefits many people is a routine that includes showing gratitude for what you have in your life. Finally, consider carving out time to meditate. This means quieting your mind of busy thoughts and focusing on a straightforward idea—like your breath. Meditation is an excellent way to practice becoming aware of the magic of the present moment.

Finding a routine that works for you is key regardless of what you decide. Document your thoughts and intentions and ways to create a safe space for spirituality in your life. And if you feel ready to do so, document your thoughts about your fears about opening yourself up to spirituality or a spiritual community. You may find answers to some of the questions you have about the absence of happiness in your life by doing this work. If you need a document to support your reflection, download the "Your Spirituality" tool found in the Spiritual Health folder at *nancysfreetools.com*.

MICRO-ACTIONS: INTERNAL REFLECTION, GRATITUDE, AND MEDITATION

Internal Reflection

Internal reflection takes conscious effort, which means making a deliberate choice and being aware of your actions. Having a prompt for reflection is very helpful, which is why a structured religious community often succeeds. The readings and reflection that typically occur as part of any religious observance provide an opportunity for reshifting your focus to what is going on in your life, how you feel about it, and the magic of being present in the moment.

Reflection is often internal but can also involve a discussion with someone else. If you aren't using the traditional religious community format, consider some options such as an online community, a support group that meets in your area, or a counsellor. Keeping your reflection to yourself might be an initial micro-action until you are able to connect with a broader community.

You can also use a journal to make a reflective entry. Reflect on your impressions of the past week. Create a framework and break your review into several focused topics: Your relationship with yourself, your relationship with your family, your thoughts about spirituality and whether you feel connected or disconnected this week. Consider the positives and the negatives of each area. Then, as you progress in this area, look back on previous weeks' entries and note any changes in focus and emotions. Create a new entry where you reflect on these changes and emotions. Did you try something new this week, like prayer or meditation? Did you consider where you are spiritually and if this is an area of your life you want to work on? How did it feel?

Internal reflection can be potent when done in the coaching environment. This can be very formal, with a defined framework, or much less structured, like a freeform discussion with a mentor. Look for these opportunities online or in your community and determine which micro-actions you can add to your life.

Gratitude

There is scientific evidence that gratitude supports your ongoing health, happiness, and well-being.

There are several ways you can work on gratitude. First, recognizing what you have and being grateful requires self-reflection and appreciation for even the little things. Taking note of the details of your life draws your awareness to how good things really are.

Gratitude also helps you see the beauty in the small things you might typically overlook—the blossoms on the trees, the easily found parking spot, and the phone call from a friend. These small acknowledgments can be just as impactful on your happiness meter as other seemingly more significant events.

The third part of the gratitude practice requires review. Looking back on your journal entries allows you to relive the experiences and release the same feel-good chemicals in your body that were released when you had the initial experience. Skeptical? Try it!

There are many ways to add the micro-action of gratitude into your life. The most challenging part is remembering to do it. For some people, it's easier to start with three things each day for which you are grateful. They don't need to be big things; little things count, like the fact that it was a sunny day, eating good food, or leaving work on time. Write them down, adding how each of them made you feel.

Of course, many other ways to bring gratitude into your life exist as well. Some people share beautiful images of the places they are visiting or things they saw in their day on social media. If this is a micro-action that is already part of your life, instead of just sharing the picture next time, add one comment about how the place makes you feel and why you are grateful for the experience. Use the words *grateful* or *gratitude* in your post.

Now, verbally express your gratitude to those you are around. In your workspace, offer an extra word of thanks to an employee or co-worker by acknowledging a job done well. Give extra praise to a service provider, and thank the salesperson for taking such good care of you. Rather than just saying thank you, be specific and explain why their effort made a difference to your experience. This doesn't just bring happiness into your life—it allows happiness to flow through you to others, making for more happiness in the world.

Meditation

The third micro-action you could incorporate into your spiritual life is meditation. Many successful people make this a part of their routine. This is an activity that takes practice and isn't an all-or-nothing sort of skill. So don't beat yourself up if you find it challenging. Learning to be present in the moment is not easy, and you will have to be patient with yourself.

My next micro-action when working on my own personal spiritual life was to download a meditation app. There are a few easy-to-use apps out there. I like "Insight Timer" because you can choose how much time you want to spend meditating and filter for a specific focus, both of which are great features for beginners. Finding a quote for the day to contemplate while meditating can be a starting point to help you positively focus your energy and offer you something to reflect on in that moment and hopefully throughout your day.

Finally, find a time when you can sit still for a few minutes without any distractions. Getting started can be challenging, so focus on doing what you can. Keeping this practice realistic is key for success in this area. Often the only reason we never start is because we feel overwhelmed before we even try. Start with one minute and take it from there.

Some people choose to end their day with meditation; others prefer the morning. Fit the micro-action into your life where you know you can make it a habit, like tacking it onto something you already do. Doing so will help you be more likely to repeat it. Remember—micro-actions stacked and celebrated are the secret to changing your life from the inside out and discovering meaningful ways to encounter and experience more happiness! You want to ensure you are going to be able to repeat the micro-actions you choose to implement into your life so that you can benefit from them.

FINANCIAL HEALTH

> *A big part of financial freedom is*
> *having your heart and mind free from*
> *worry about the what-ifs of life.*
> — SUZE ORMAN

Before diving into your financial health, remember to start with the "Continuum Tool" to help you reflect on what you are moving away from and toward in this area. The scenarios that you generate using the tool will help you connect with the emotions associated with each situation. These emotions become the motivation needed to propel you away from the pain of the worst-case situation and toward the pleasure of the best-case situation to reprioritize your spiritual health. It is through these intentional micro-actions that you cultivate greater happiness.

By getting a better idea of the best- and worst-case scenarios, you will also be able to outline your goal for financial health. Determining what this goal is will be your first micro-action. You can then use this larger goal to help you create smaller, more manageable micro-actions that can be incorporated into your life with far more ease. Remember to refer to "The Importance of Goals and Creating a Plan" in Part One for creating a plan

for success, and remember to download the "Goals," "Scheduling," and "Habits" resources from *nancysfreetools.com* to dive more deeply. Through these intentional micro-actions, you will build momentum and create a life that brings you happiness.

KNOW WHAT YOU CAN CONTROL

Money is one of the most common fears shared among human beings—more specifically, the fear related to financial insecurity, which can feel like a direct threat to our well-being as well as that of our families. Given that money is crucial for our survival and success in the modern world, can you ever really be free of this worry?

You might believe that getting more money would resolve this worry, but this is a common myth. You take yourself with you wherever you go; this means that you carry whatever beliefs were formed in your childhood with you into the various other stages of your life. Fears don't automatically disappear—they need to be challenged and reframed, so even if you are a person who grew up without financial security but you're now financially stable, your beliefs about money may still be the same. Having more money changes your financial position but it won't take away your fears.

So many people seem to have been conditioned to fear the loss of money and focus on the what-ifs—experiences from their lives based on their socioeconomic conditions or how their families modeled financial health. These experiences lead to assumptions about money and drive the underlying beliefs about making, having, losing, and keeping money. The result is behaviors that are either productive or counterproductive to your relationship with money, leading to a constant state of vigilance and heightened alertness, which creates a feedback loop that perpetuates more worry.

It's a vicious cycle.

To stop this, you need to focus on what you can control. When the worry pops up, focus on which emotions are associated with the concern and then try to understand what experiences led to the assumptions driving those emotions.

Is your assumption that there is not enough, and you won't be able to meet your or your family's basic needs? This survival response is likely heightened if you grew up with food or financial insecurity. If you assume you will eventually lose your job or your family's livelihood, perhaps it's due to growing up in an economic crisis and watching people lose everything they had worked for.

Unfortunately, these experiences can lead to persistent worry and stress. They will likely lead to assumptions about yourself, the world, and money that no longer serve you and that hamper your ability to develop financial confidence which will affect your experience of overall happiness.

The first micro-action you can take to establish more self-assurance in this area is to start becoming aware of what experiences and assumptions about money you have brought with you into your adult life. How did your parents or caregivers talk about money? What emotions did you experience when money was being discussed in your home—either because you asked for money or because a discussion about money was going on around you? What kind of language was used in your home when money was discussed—were they words of scarcity, fear, or anger? How have the experiences and language of your childhood shaped the financial landscape of your adult life? Journal your thoughts.

Now that you are starting to develop awareness around your financial assumptions, it is essential to focus away from the worry and toward what you can control.

The next micro-action is to think about what you can manage now, today, or this week regarding the finances in your life. What is critical? What can you control right now? If you can't change what's happening, work hard to take it off that day's worry list by practicing one of the other micro-actions you have learned in this book: meditation or being mindfully present in the moment.

Meditation and mindfulness are great ways to ease worry and anxiety. The "Insight Timer" meditation app allows you to search for particular focus areas. Consider searching "money" and finding meditation topics that provide money affirmations, mantras, or meditations to ease worry or stress around money.

If you can control some aspect of what's happening financially, that's what you do. This could be putting a small amount of money into a savings account, paying a bill, or making a small payment toward your credit card. What matters is that you do *something*; move forward with the next micro-action that is in your control. This is hard work and requires courage and consistency, but you will have much greater peace of mind and problem-solve more successfully using this technique.

An easy-to-understand example of how this works is when the bills to be paid are bigger than the dollars in the bank account. You could worry until this issue is resolved by itself (unlikely) or look at the situation and decide on the micro-actions you can take to solve the problem yourself. Maybe that micro-action is paying only some of the bills or a portion of each of the bills, then determining how to reduce spending until more funds are available. Consistently practice this micro-action after every payday and you will start to see a difference—not only in your finances, but in your ability to face the challenge head-on rather than avoid it!

A healthy way to manage this is to accept that all possible micro-actions have been taken, you have done what you can for now, and these micro-actions count. Your thoughts now need to be focused on other areas until funds are available again and you can consider the next micro-actions. This isn't easy, but it will lead to greater financial health and create a path to future happiness.

INCOME, EXPENSES, AND DOCUMENTATION

The next micro-action I recommend for better financial health can be broken down into two parts of an equation: income and expenses.

Income means what you earn. What money is incoming in your life? Expenses mean the things in your life that are costing you. What do you pay for? When these two components are balanced—when what you earn equals what you spend—you are breaking even. This is called a balance sheet. As an adult, you have likely gone through this balancing experience at least once. If it wasn't a process you initiated yourself, then maybe it occurred when you completed a loan application. In most cases, it is a rather distressing process that spells out exactly where you are financially. In order to achieve greater financial health, you need to do a balance sheet of your financial life as it currently looks.

Create a balance sheet of your finances. The more detail you include in your balance sheet, the more valuable your work will be. You may discover that you are not where you want to be right now. This micro-action will often reveal that you have too much debt, but it can also be a helpful micro-action for determining how long it will take you to pay for your debt using your current payment practices. Again, this can be a stressful practice, but I highly recommend it.

Remember to examine your experiences and assumptions, identify the emotions connected to these, and intentionally shift your focus away from the worry to what you can control. Avoiding your financial situation out of fear will not fix this area of your life, but taking the next micro-action will eventually lead you out of insecurity and into your economic power. Debt might be your reality today, but working to reduce and limit your debt in the future is the objective.

Documenting your finances accurately to create total transparency of your financial situation will allow you to get to a point where you can have the freedom to choose—to a certain extent—how much you would like to spend instead of mindlessly spending all the money you have, or even more than you earn. This is true for whatever economic level you are at.

Most people react to an increase in income with an increase in spending. It's crucial to readjust your behavior to spend below your current income. This will mean making sacrifices! But there is no shortcut around this without getting into more debt. Over time, you can work to increase your income and with it, your lifestyle. However, no matter your income level, you will always need to be aware of your balance sheet to be confident that you are spending below your income.

The micro-actions for this practice look like writing down every single expense you have. With infinite time, you would try to record everything for a whole year. However, you at least want to start by recording everything for a month. Most people work paycheck-to-paycheck or monthly since many recurring expenses like car payments, rent or mortgage, and utilities occur monthly.

The next micro-action is to write down your exact income. Don't say about $500 per week; you should document the exact number, for example $497.67, on your last paycheck.

Use your previous documentation of how you spend each one of those dollars to determine how much of your income you spend over the next month. When you have a month of income and expenses, you will have completed step one of creating financial health. To make this easier for you, I have created the "Understanding Your Numbers" tool and the "Being Really Honest" tool—both found in the Financial Health folder at *nancysfreetools.com*.

BUDGET

Creating your budget means using your monthly expenses, adding them up, and determining how many leftover dollars you have at the end of the month. For many, there are no leftover dollars at the end of the month, and that's why so many people have excessive debt.

This is why the previous micro-actions require full transparency. You must be able to say, "My paycheck is $498.10, but every month I spend $510." Now you have a clear representation of how much debt you are accumulating every month. This might be the wake-up call you need to execute the necessary micro-actions and call attention to possible beliefs and behaviors that are holding you back from experiencing happiness—financial and otherwise.

The purpose of this micro-action is not to overwhelm you, but if you have determined that financial happiness is an important area of focus in your life, you must be willing to do the work. Money makes people emotional. This is normal!

This may not be how you had expected your life or financial situation to look, and you may feel you have let yourself or your family down. However, these feelings should not determine what you do next. They are likely connected to limiting behaviors and beliefs that got you here in the first place. Feel them, label them, understand where they come from, but be willing to let them go while still doing the next right micro-action. You can't wait until everything is perfect or you feel better before you're willing to take the first step. You must start where you are—this is how you change your life.

You are not a failure and you do not need to feel ashamed of your life or financial situation. You have done the best you can with what you had, and sometimes what you had was terrible. Start showing yourself compassion for the choices you made that you believed were right for you at the time.

Anxiety associated with money may never go away for you, but you can learn how to feel the emotion without it controlling your next decision. You don't need to wait for the uncomfortable emotions to pass before you make changes in this or any other area.

Look honestly at your budget. You can now clearly see how far behind you are falling each month. Ideally, you want to have items on the expense side that include things like savings, retirement funds, and emergency accounts. Even if your contributions to these special areas are modest, the micro-actions in this area really do add up.

Once you recognize where you are, you can make a better plan for where you are going.

Your next micro-action in Step Two is to decrease your spending or increase your income, although reducing your spending is probably more realistic for most people. Identify leaks you can plug, like buying takeaway coffees, takeout meals, or clothes. Start cooking at home! Whatever you need to do to decrease your spending, ideally, you will get to a point where you have matched your budget and created a bit of a cushion, maybe as much as twenty percent of your income.

Find somewhere safe to put the extra dollars. Maybe your safe spot will be in a separate bank account, a piggy bank, or an envelope in your sock drawer. Wherever it is, make sure it's not too easy for you to access. The idea is to put this money away and not touch it. The purpose is to start reducing stress and empowering yourself with as little as a few dollars every month. And you will need to practice!

If your financial situation is seriously out of balance, consider seeking assistance from a professional. There are many excellent professionals, some of whom even offer this assistance free of charge. Whether you are just starting and want to create a sound financial plan as your earnings increase, or you are trying to juggle acquired credit card and educational debt, or you are trying to conceive how to design your financial future to allow for a purchase like a home, there are advisors trained to assist you at every stage of life.

Planning is key to your financial success and ultimate independence. It is never too early to seek guidance. The sooner you take these steps, the easier your financial life will become.

Until you clearly know where you are, there is no way you can plan a path to implement micro-actions that will change your current financial picture. Micro-actions in this area can make all the difference. If you have access to a financial advisor, this can be an excellent micro-action to help get you started. If you don't have access to a financial advisor either through your bank or otherwise, get recommendations from those in your circle who appear to have achieved greater economic independence. That might be a supervisor, a family friend, or even someone who is recommended to you by another professional.

There are also educational tools, books, and videos that can support you in this process and ultimately assist you unlocking financial freedom and embracing the happiness that comes with it.

If there are people in your life that you are responsible for—a partner, children, aging parents—life insurance is also a sensible micro-action to consider with your extra dollars.

When you are young and in good health, this can be very inexpensive and offer significant security. It is a way to support those you leave behind if something were to happen to you prematurely.

Many people avoid this as part of their plan for financial security because they don't like thinking about their mortality. But financial health includes facing these uncomfortable emotions and remembering that you don't make yourself happier by avoiding the inevitable or trying to control life. Instead, you need to intentionally decide that you are going to do the work to find happiness in the midst of the uncertainty and with the knowledge that everything can change in an instant.

Another micro-action to consider taking in the area of financial health is having a will.

A will is a legal document outlining how you want your assets distributed after death. This can provide peace of mind and prevent emotional and financial strain on your loved ones after your death.

Lawyers can be expensive, but managing the loss of a loved one without a will in place can be financially devastating. If you do not have a will, your assets will be distributed according to law, which may not align with your wishes and may leave the people who rely on you with little to no financial security. Ask around for recommendations for a lawyer who has helped people you trust so that you can ensure you are taken care of according to your individual needs. It can be a critical help for those left behind.

Along with life insurance and a will, you should make clear what your wishes would be if you can't make medical decisions for yourself. This can be done with a document typically called an advance directive or a living will and plays a crucial role in personal autonomy, giving you peace of mind knowing that if you are ever incapacitated and unable to make decisions for yourself, your wishes will be carried out. Sample advance directives can be found online.

You could consider financial micro-actions for those around you, such as your children. One of them is an education fund, and it is a great way to set aside funds for expensive educational costs that are likely to present themselves in the future.

Even the most modest contributions compound over the years and can mean the difference between financial freedom or debt for your children. This can even be a fund that others contribute to as a gift for your children on their birthdays or for celebrations, and can be set up in their names.

Practicing micro-actions that promote happiness is a skill you can model for your children through every decision and choice you take, including financial micro-actions. Financial freedom is a gift you can leave for the generations to come.

FAMILY

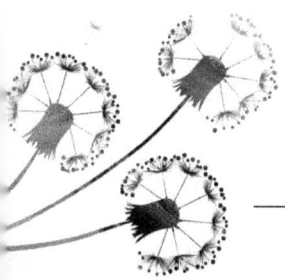

Family is not an important thing.
It's everything.
— MICHAEL J. FOX

Before diving into your work on family, remember to start with the "Continuum Tool" available at *nancysfreetools.com* to help you reflect on what you are moving away from and toward in this area. The scenarios that you generate using the tool will help you connect with the emotions associated with each situation. These emotions become the motivation needed to propel you away from the pain of the worst-case situation and toward the pleasure of the best-case situation to reprioritize your family. It is through these intentional micro-actions that you cultivate greater happiness.

By getting a better idea of the best- and worst-case scenarios, you will also be able to outline your goal for family. Determining what this goal is will be your first micro-action. You can then use this larger goal to help you create smaller, more manageable micro-actions that can be incorporated into your life with far more ease. Remember to refer to "The Importance of Goals and Creating a Plan" in Part One for creating a plan for success, and

remember to download the "Goals," "Scheduling," and "Habits" resources from *nancysfreetools.com* to dive more deeply. Through these intentional micro-actions, you will build momentum and create a life that brings you happiness.

FAMILY: WHO ARE THEY?

No matter your experience, you probably have some relationship with a group of people you consider family. Even if you have different birth parents or have lost connection with birth families, there is usually a circle of people around you that fit into this label, even if it's unconventional.

You can frame family in several ways.

Traditionally, there are the parents and grandparents who influenced your youth, the extended family members and close family friends who impacted your young adult years, the family you married into, and the family you built with your partner. Family may even extend to include school, neighborhood, and sports communities that have played a significant role in your life.

The micro-actions in this chapter can be modified and applied to any relationship, no matter its nature. The following section relates to immediate family relationships.

Your immediate family can be defined as your parents, your siblings, and your children. These principles can also be extended to include divorced and blended families.

Let's first focus on your parents. Many people have strained relationships with their parents, and do not value doing work in this area. That is fine, but consider if it will help your other relationships.

If you want to understand the landscape of all your current and past relationships, starting at the beginning is key. Your experiences with your parents have shaped you and your worldview; this includes your assumptions about other people and your expectations of how relationships are supposed to look. These assumptions can significantly affect your ability to experience happiness in relationships, so there is considerable value in starting here.

Start by determining your baseline before you choose how much time to dedicate to building your relationships. This is hard work, and your decisions are often clouded by your emotions—what you think you should be doing or what you think others will say about what you are doing.

A large part of this work is giving yourself permission to have your emotions about these relationships, understanding how your experiences have influenced these emotions, and allowing yourself to make choices based on your priorities

If your parents are no longer alive or able to interact with you, please continue with this exercise and modify it as you need to. Sometimes, pain previously not managed in person can still be managed through reflection. These micro-actions don't require the participation of your parents to have a positive outcome.

The first micro-action that helps you work toward healing and discovering greater happiness in this area is taking responsibility for your role in your unhappiness. Most people create a lot of baggage over their lifetimes and blame their childhood experiences for most of the baggage. Taking responsibility for past mistakes is difficult, but the truth is that much of the baggage you carry is a responsibility you share with your parents.

It might be classified as blame, but it is healthier and less confrontational to refer to it as responsibility. So, although placing blame on people or circumstances of the past is very common and sometimes very necessary, it is good to consider a different perspective or to determine whether continuing to carry the baggage is keeping you from happiness.

Are there assumptions you are carrying around about yourself and the world based on experiences with your parents? What are these assumptions? Whatever they are, try to reframe these thoughts to recognize that your parents and experiences may have challenged you, whether intended or not, but this has allowed you to grow and made you who you are today.

Taking responsibility for your role in your happiness does not mean you are responsible for any abuse or neglect that was inflicted on you as a child or at any point in your life where you were powerless. This pain is valid and deserves healing, but often that healing starts with exploring the ways continuing to carry that pain is hindering you from experiencing true happiness now. Most of us won't receive the kind of love or apology we long for from the people who hurt us, but we can choose a life that is not determined by these past experiences. This is where true power and happiness lie.

Take a moment to reflect inwardly on your relationship with your parents or caregivers. Use your journal to document your experiences and any emotions that arise while reflecting. What assumptions have you drawn about yourself and relationships based on the one you have with your parents and the one they have with each other? Are you able to look at the relationship from the other person's perspective? What do you see if you put yourself in their shoes? Is there a way you can reframe these experiences so that they hurt a bit less? This doesn't excuse any harm done to you, but it can help you start the process of letting go and finding freedom from this pain.

Writing is a tool used less and less these days, but it is proven to help your subconscious process what you are reflecting on by reorganizing thoughts and promoting critical thinking. Writing also allows you to become aware of patterns, and awareness of relationship patterns is crucial to working toward greater happiness in the area of personal relationships by reworking complicated and complex emotions and personal experiences into smaller, more manageable parts. It will also help you change the narrative of your life and help you see the resilience you have already displayed through hardship. Discovering you are braver and stronger than you ever thought is a transformative passage toward happiness.

The result of putting memories and feelings into words, processing them as you do so, is that you reduce the intensity of those memories and emotions and allow yourself to grieve. This is how to start to make space in your life for something new, even if it's just a new approach to old relationships.

PERSPECTIVES

Whether it is a relationship with your parents, siblings, or even your children, practicing inward reflection and developing an awareness of the value these connections bring to your life is essential to experiencing happiness. Understanding your history, past experiences, and assumptions based on these experiences will help you change your relationship dynamics and empower yourself to build relationships that make you feel happy—intentionally.

So why should you take the time to focus on your relationship with your parents? Societal expectations can guilt you into feeling that you need to be kind to your parents just because they are your parents, but in order to gain anything from this inward reflection, you will need to dig deeper than guilt and obligation.

More and more Western societies are drifting away from multigenerational homes and communities. There are more retirement communities than ever, and fewer families choosing to care for aging parents. This shift is creating an information gap that perpetuates a cycle of the loss of generational knowledge and perspectives.

Whether it is your own parents or other people similar in age to your parents, consider the value of exposure to different generations for yourself and your children. You may joke and laugh about the stories your parents tell of life "when they were young" and how hard they had it, but this perspective is important to incorporate into your own understanding of the world and your children's.

Having your perspectives reframed by your parents or people from their generation can help change your assumptions about others and the world. It can help you redefine what you think happiness is supposed to be by giving you an opportunity to observe your life objectively and practice gratitude—even if it's just for the advances in society that have afforded you and your children more freedom and opportunities. Listening to your parents share their own stories can also help you understand why they made the decisions they made when you were growing up, which will likely allow you to experience compassion for them, a vast difference for so many people whose dominant emotion when it comes to their parents is anger.

While respect isn't necessarily just granted to people because of their age, you will gain far more in life—and experience far more happiness—by having an open mind and considering perspectives that differ from yours. This opens the door to critical thinking and problem solving, soft skills that are crucial for not only survival in the modern world, but thriving in the modern world.

If you are not on good terms with your parents or your parents have died, but you still want to learn what other generations have to offer, interact with an older generation. Visit a retirement facility to spend time with the people there, offering to volunteer or share a skill, or visit a friend's parents.

No matter what your life situation looks like, there are many ways to open yourself up to surrogate relationships that can be very healing.

The wisdom of older generations is a treasure trove of lessons, but you need not put yourself in harm's way to receive it. Find people you can safely spend time with and listen to their experiences. Remember—working toward happiness is about changing how you see the world! You might think your life is unique, but you will be surprised to learn how much life occurs in cycles.

Relationships Change Over Time

Relationships change over time, and your experiences and assumptions about your memory of many events are unlikely to be completely accurate. This is true for all relationships but seems particularly pronounced for childhood relationships.

Childhood memories are formed at a time when your understanding of the world is still developing. Different developmental stages influence how you interpret experiences based on what you understand about yourself, your immediate family, and the world at that time. Your memories will also be subjective, and this can affect your recollection of events.

This explains why some of your childhood memories differ from the same memories your siblings or parents may have.

Memory is also not concrete and can become distorted throughout your life based on storytelling and new experiences. Thus, faulty memories will impact your relationship with your family because you may recall very different experiences. But, this malleability also means you can reframe the story you are telling yourself about your life.

For your next micro-action, take a few moments to travel back in time and reflect on some childhood memories and how your relationships have changed over your lifetime based on your experiences and assumptions and the emotions associated with these assumptions.

Choose one of your parental relationships and practice internal reflection on this relationship during your time in high school. How did you view your parents at that time? Did you value their experience? What happened to this relationship as you moved into your twenties? Do you remember or know what changed?

What is important is that you realize that relationships change over time because people change, and how you relate to others also starts to change as you mature. Consider the power of what you choose to focus on when reflecting on this relationship. What is the story you are telling yourself about this person? What words do you use to describe this relationship?

Consider what micro-action you can take to start changing this story. Is it shifting the language from "controlling" to "caring"? Is it reframing your parents saying no to understanding that they may not have had the money for what you were asking for? Did they have personal issues with their own parents that could have shaped the way they raised you? Shift your focus to consider alternate perspectives, and watch as your emotions shift with this awareness.

This same exercise can be used for your relationship with your siblings. There is value in understanding the memories you have regarding your sibling relationships, how they have shaped you, and how you relate to people in current relationships because of them.

It is one thing to have an experience and hold an assumption about an event; it is quite another thing to be able to share those experiences and to relive them with a sibling. Some of these experiences may be what are considered "family secrets," and a sibling is the only other person you feel comfortable sharing the details of those memories with, allowing you to work through traumatic experiences and process certain assumptions and emotions that have been difficult to process up until now.

Being able to step back and understand the view of either an older sibling or a younger sibling may give you more information to gain a deeper understanding of many of your life experiences. It could be as simple as starting a conversation with your sibling or reflecting on family secrets in your journal. Remember, starting small is key.

When attempting these micro-actions, if you feel safe doing so, ask a number of people about their memories and emotions of the same event. Try to look at it as a way to understand why their experiences of the event may differ from yours. Was it their state of mind? Their relationship with the people involved? Their assumptions? This helps you to understand how every experience is open to interpretation based on each person's expectations and worldview and how your life is impacted by the assumptions you have drawn.

So why is reflecting on the past useful? How can that really help you in the future?

Reflection allows you to notice progress and to use new information to consider old details. This means you can focus on how you and the other person have grown and how life experiences have shaped new worldviews.

Even in situations where the relationship has deteriorated, reflect on times when your relationship was stronger. It could be physical proximity that helped to keep the relationship alive or a shared community or activity that gave you relatability. Whatever it was that made you feel closer to this person, it is that time that is valuable to reflect on. What emotions do you associate with your time with this person? How have these emotions changed? How has your focus in the area of this relationship shifted? Journal about this reflection.

Reflect on those different phases of life and document your emotions about your relationships. Now, imagine what the ideal relationship with each of these people would look like. What do you wish these relationships were like? Consider using the "Relationship Reflection" tool in the Family folder to dig a bit deeper into your impressions of your relationships with family.

Additional documentation can be done using the "Continuum Tool." Remember, the "Continuum Tool" is designed to help you understand the current situation, the worst-case scenario in this area, and then the best-case scenario in this area. Sibling relationships ebb and flow more since your time with them covers broader stages of life and development, so let's use these relationships for our example.

Reflecting on when things changed can make it easier to understand when the changes were based on circumstances out of your control and not on the assumptions you have made based on the change. This awareness, like awareness in your relationship with your parents, can change the negative emotions associated with your sibling and potentially allow for a "reset."

To further help you come up with the best-case scenario, recall a time when you really enjoyed time with a sibling and did something fun. Now, think about what made that experience memorable.

Now, using the "Continuum Tool," generate a version of reality that describes the worst description of this relationship—a situation that would represent pain and something you want to avoid. Remember, the brain moves away from pain and toward pleasure, so this micro-action is about rewiring your brain to seek out the ideal relationship and avoid the worst possible outcome, assisting you in your efforts to enter into more meaningful relationships with your loved ones and hopefully rekindle the happiness these relationships used to bring you, or, at the very least, the possibility of happiness in the future.

CHILDREN & PARENTING

Not only do healthy relationships with your parents and siblings improve your life and allow you to experience more happiness, but they can also cultivate more positive relationships with your own children and grandchildren.

Exploring thoughts and ideas about child-rearing practices can be controversial. Discussions around what is the right way to raise children can quickly become heated. So, who's to say what's right and wrong?

There isn't a right way to resolve any issue. Usually, there are many "right ways," and context is essential. Every situation is different. There are a few absolutes and almost always more information that can alter your perspective if you are open to hearing it.

Advice is a tricky thing. It is crucial to quiet the little voice in your head and the loud voices outside your head and trust an ancient source: your deeper consciousness. You need to move forward with the micro-actions that support your belief system and are aligned with your priorities.

Many parents feel torn between what they would like to do for their children and what they think they should be doing, particularly women who want to spend time with their children but also want to return to work when their children are young. Your experiences will shape your assumptions and help you determine what happiness could look like in this area.

KNOW YOUR STARTING POINT

The micro-actions in this area will prompt you to self-reflect and draw your own conclusions about how to add value to your parenting techniques to develop the kind of relationship you would like with your children while maintaining alignment with your priorities.

Learning to feel comfortable with your choices takes practice.

Early in your parenting life, it will be easy to be swayed by the opinions of others; however, with experience and time, you will gradually learn to trust your heart and believe in yourself and that you know your child best. These traits will serve you as you work to become increasingly more comfortable with your choices.

Sometimes, the necessary work comes in the form of inward reflection, which helps you better understand your motivation for making your decisions. Are you holding onto a belief or convention because it's always been done that way, or are your reasons based on knowledge about your children and on your own experiences with them?

Children need a relatively predictable life; they need consistency and reliability. Knowing what will happen daily allows them to develop secure attachments and feel safe enough to be curious and explore the world. Something as simple as being available for them and ensuring regular time spent connecting makes them emotionally healthier.

If you are not happy with your current relationship with your children or your availability for them, start your micro-actions as soon as you can because they aren't going to be young and in your home forever. Consider a simple start: reevaluate your priorities and reframe spending time with your children or being available for them as your choice.

Change can be as simple as deciding you *want* to spend time with your children rather than you *have* to.

Living with your choices becomes easier once you have done the inward reflection and you can better understand your heart. By using emotional reflection practices, you can understand the feelings you attach to the micro-actions, decisions, or choices you make with your children.

Using this awareness, ask yourself how these experiences will shape your children's assumptions and worldview in the future. How will the micro-actions you take today shape the future of your children's experiences of happiness?

DOCUMENTATION OF THE DETAILS
AND THE FEELINGS

So, how do you spend more time with your children? The secret to experiencing greater happiness with your children is realizing that it isn't always about spending more time; it's about spending better time. The micro-actions in this area are about finding ways to change the quality of your time with them.

To start, determine your baseline. Document the time you spend with your children, whether it's high-quality or otherwise. Similarly to how you have documented how you spend your personal time, you'll want to document what you do weekly and daily with your children. The time should be documented and qualified as best as you can, down to the minute. Include the experience and your emotions regarding the experience.

Remember—this requires radical honesty and raw internal reflection. If you aren't able to be honest about how you feel about your life with your children, you will never find out what micro-actions you need to take to experience the sincere happiness you long for.

Reframe these experiences and see them from your children's point of view. You could be shuttling a car full of kids, or you could be driving just one. The latter might qualify as quality interaction, but not the former. Context matters. Either way, you need to document the time spent as you spent it and the emotions you experienced.

The next micro-action is to do internal reflection and find where you are now on the "Continuum Tool" and where you want to go. Work toward seeing how time and experiences could be reframed as quality time and how you can be more engaged in the magic of being present with your children.

It could be as simple as avoiding your phone when you are spending quality time with them. This will help you to remain engaged and focus on making them feel seen and heard.

IS IT WORTH THIS WORK?

You may ask yourself if doing the documentation is worth the time. Wouldn't getting a general idea and using the extra time to work on the changes be easier?

That may be true. It does take a significant amount of time to do the documentation using the tools, but it will be time well spent, and you won't need to keep doing it—it's a once-off exercise.

Most people have ineffective memories, particularly when it comes to documenting their time. Even if you aren't aware of it, you may under-measure or over-measure, but the result is the same: you're usually inaccurate about how much time you spend doing what.

While it's valuable to determine what you intend to do or how you intend to spend your time in the future, your most worthwhile micro-action is to measure what you actually do during the course of an average seven-day period. You need to document how those minutes were spent and the frequency of those activities.

Each child is different, so taking micro-actions that allow you to make quality time mutually beneficial will depend on each child. It doesn't need to be extensive, costly, or time-consuming. Most children, even if they don't verbalize it, appreciate one-on-one time with their parents if it's doing something they like.

It could be playing a game, shopping, or enjoying a sporting event together. A few minutes of undivided time, allowing you to experience your child and who they are, will create lifelong bonds and open the door to more meaningful conversations in the future.

VISUALIZE THE OBJECTIVE

Objectives are your big-picture goals. They shift your focus to increase more of what you want—in this case, quality time and engagement with your children. Visualizing an objective—such as the idea of having an open and reciprocal relationship with your teenager—is powerful.

How do you visualize? To ensure you take micro-actions that lead to more happiness, a vision needs to be dramatic—on either end of the spectrum.

The more dramatic the vision you can visualize, the stronger the impact will be on the subconscious. The stronger the effect on the subconscious, the more likely it is that your focus will go where you want it to go, allowing you to fully experience the beauty of your life.

However, making it realistic enough to fit into your world is still important.

You may think an open and reciprocal relationship with your child is just a fantasy, but by taking micro-actions toward a better relationship, happiness is ultimately achievable. Children, particularly teenagers, likely won't share all their deepest, darkest secrets with you, so don't expect them to, but celebrate any moments of connection you do have.

Remember, you need to break an objective down into micro-actions that can be achieved daily. In doing this, you may look back one day and realize you've achieved what initially seemed impossible.

Let's start with an example. Let's assume that you're only spending ten minutes a day with your teenage child, and that child does not appreciate the time you spend with them. The first micro-action you can take here is to determine what the issue is. The second micro-action is to decide what would be a better way to spend time together.

Consider your individual child and work with what you know about them and their energy levels throughout the day. Consider asking them what they would like to do with you—you'll likely be surprised by their answer and enthusiasm!

WAYS TO CONNECT

As children get older and become increasingly independent, finding imaginative opportunities to connect with them becomes more challenging. When integrating micro-actions into this area of your life, try to look for and be open to ways to connect with them on their terms.

This technique has helped me keep the pathways open with my children. Sometimes, this means showing interest in things that are important to them and not of much significance to me. This might be something as simple as taking an interest in their favorite video game, talking about the books they are reading, or something more involved, such as attending a sporting event or music concert of their choice.

Each child is an individual, so each opportunity to connect will likely be unique to that child. The interest needs to be genuine to be effective, but the work is worth it.

While you may not have a genuine interest in the activity, you do have a genuine interest in your child, how they engage in that activity, and what their thoughts are about it, and this is what counts. Being present in these moments with them will allow you to cultivate authentic connection and happiness. You may need to fake it a bit in the beginning, but the love is real! And that's okay.

This really is the key to a sustainable relationship with your children—and experiencing more happiness overall.

The effort shows your respect for them and their interests, which is essential for continued growth in the relationship. Sometimes, you may genuinely share a common interest, and that makes it easier. But connecting over things you don't share an interest in can sometimes be even more impactful, and letting your child teach you about their passion may increase their respect for you.

Learning from your children and understanding their unique interests and skills can be enlightening.

You might decide to spend time with your child, offering your undivided attention, and asking them questions about what they want to do, what they feel they are good at, and how they would like to spend time together. You could stack this with a micro-action like suppressing the desire to teach them and allowing them to be the expert! This involves more "not doing" than doing.

Whatever micro-action you choose to do next in your relationship with your children, the key is to make sure that you are showing up to be a part of their lives. The rest will follow.

PARTNER

> *Be willing to share all of who you are.*
> *So many of us want a partner,*
> *but we're not willing to show all of us.*
> — Iyanla Vanzant

Before diving into your relationship with your partner, remember to start with the "Continuum Tool" to help you reflect on what you are moving away from and toward in this area. The scenarios that you generate using the tool will help you connect with the emotions associated with each situation. These emotions become the motivation needed to propel you away from the pain of the worst-case situation and toward the pleasure of the best-case situation to reprioritize your partner in your life. It is through these intentional micro-actions that you cultivate greater happiness.

By getting a better idea of the best- and worst-case scenarios, you will also be able to outline your goal for working on goals related to your partner. Determining what this goal is will be your first micro-action. You can then use this larger goal to help you create smaller, more manageable micro-actions that can be incorporated into your life with far more ease. Remember to refer to "The Importance of Goals and Creating a Plan" in

Part One for creating a plan for success, and remember to download the "Goals," "Scheduling," and "Habits" resources from *nancysfreetools.com* to dive more deeply. Through these intentional micro-actions, you will build momentum and create a life that brings you happiness.

IMPRESSION AND VALUE OF YOUR RELATIONSHIP

You are likely right if you think you need to give this particular area of your life more attention.

If you feel everything is okay in this area, it may be. But would your partner agree with you? If you feel your partner would say that you are only doing okay, then maybe you need to do some internal reflection.

If this is resonating with you, don't ignore it.

Of course, this is a delicate subject. Most trained professionals spend long hours trying to unravel the mysteries of romantic relationships. I am not pretending for a second that I am a marriage counselor or an expert or even that my marriage was ideal. The only message that is important for me to relay in this chapter is that it is not about what "they" do. It is about what *you* do.

Working hard to experience more happiness in your relationships, whether with your kids, friends, siblings, or partner, is all about what micro-actions you choose to take and what emotions you choose to feel about your behaviors. You have the power to make your relationships better.

Of course, the participation of your partner will greatly increase the quality of this work and lead to a deeper connection and experience of happiness in this area, but you can do a lot by just changing your awareness, attitude, and expectations through the micro-actions you take because of them.

One of the micro-actions that has worked for me is exploring Love Languages, a concept popularized by Gary Chapman, who writes in easy-to-understand language and shares wonderful real-life stories that clearly explain the love languages related to spousal love and family relationships. His focus is all about taking control of your own micro-actions, being conscious and intentional with your focus, and understanding the other person's needs first.

Often, in a relationship, people tend to only think of their own needs, the things they want, and the things their significant other does for them—and that is where they start their complaints and try to make changes. If this sounds like your life, you will not attain happiness with your partner if you continue. Remember—happiness is not about balancing and controlling people, places, or things outside of you; it is about doing the work from within—no matter what is going on externally.

What does it take to find a life partner? Is it about finding? Or is it really about being open enough to receive when the right person is nearby? I am a believer in the latter, which is about receiving. However, to be present in the moment of arrival and able to receive this person into your life, you need to know yourself. You must be open enough to honestly share who you are—the good and the bad.

Different life experiences will bring different partners. There are always the "fun ones." These people introduce you to exciting things, but may not be so good at considering the needs of others. Then there are the "nice ones." They are usually really good at considering the needs of others, but might not be so exciting.

Some potential partners may think you are perfect just the way you are, and others might push you to do things that you never thought you'd be able to do. Finding happiness in the area of partnership is about finding the right combination of these qualities that bring about the right match for you. That is the greatest secret. Of course, there might need to be some chemistry, too!

The secret to fulfilling relationships starts with the relationship you have with yourself. Maybe you are good at internal reflection and have insight into who you are and what you want, or like me, you figured it out by experimenting with different relationships throughout your life, which eventually helped me better understand myself. Whatever it is, it is important to realize that understanding your needs for a relationship does not always align with what your friends and family might think you need.

I remember when I was first engaged to my husband, my friends were very forthcoming in suggesting my husband-to-be wasn't "nice enough" to me. As well as they knew me, I understood my own motivations better than they did. He challenged me to reach my potential in ways no one else was able to. Our depth of understanding and how to support one another was often unspoken, and it worked for us. I think that he really believed I could read his mind, and in many cases, maybe I could.

If you are struggling in your relationships, I want to say that if you love someone very much, it is definitely worth working through your differences. Take the necessary micro-actions in this area. Determine your Love Language, and use your words to show appreciation for one another. Use your words to say sorry and shift your relationship's narrative to cultivate love and respect.

The key here is that the micro-actions you take must serve your partnership —not others. Don't look to others to determine what works for you; practice internal reflection and determine your relationship needs.

Finding someone who sees your potential and encourages you to excel really makes for a strong, lasting relationship. Your spouse, your companion, your mate, your soulmate; for most people, this is one of the most significant relationships in their lives. Unfortunately, this is often the person who gets the least attention.

Most people know how to make someone feel special, acknowledge their love and appreciation, and recognize them. However, when you truly reflect, you are probably guilty of not focusing on your relationship and showing your appreciation to your partner because other things are always in the way. People believe that those closest to them don't need to be reminded of how much they are loved, but they do, because all human beings do, usually more than they will ever share.

It is not that you need to spend every waking moment thinking about your partner, but it is probably the one area of your life that isn't prioritized as much as it should be.

The most potent micro-action you can take in this area is to wake up that feeling of desire again. Every person needs to feel desirable, appreciated, and loved. Some argue it is really what makes us "tick." Can you recall the magic moments in the early parts of your relationship? Do you remember feeling happy? You can work toward more satisfaction in your relationship by focusing on recreating these experiences and emotions.

Another significant micro-action you can take in your relationship is to spend some time journaling about your partner. What do you appreciate about them? What emotions do you remember from when you first met? Do you still experience those emotions now? When? What do you think you can say more often to them? What do you think they would appreciate hearing?

IT'S ALL ABOUT YOUR VIEW

If you can get yourself to what may seem like a rather altruistic place, maybe a place more like you were in when you were first dating, you may be much more successful in your pursuit of experiencing happiness in your relationship.

The objective is to take yourself to a place where you want to consider the needs of the other person. You may even have to appear to be making an effort with this behavior for now; we can call this "acting" if you like! Still, if you can do this, you may get to a point where you start to feel that you really do want to do this behavior out of love and not as a performance.

Consider the following questions in a journal reflection or by using "The Perfect Partner" or "Your Perspective" tools in the Partner folder at *nancysfreetools.com*. What past experiences, including your relationship with your parents and their marriage, have shaped your assumptions about a partner? How does this impact your happiness today? How does this awareness shift your perspective of your partner and allow you to stop living through an outdated narrative?

So what would "acting" look like? Let's say you know the other person loves it when you welcome them home, but it might feel out of character to drop what you are doing and greet them at the door. Try to do this micro-action anyway, and be as authentic as possible. This micro-action works at cultivating the feeling you believe they are longing for from you, and their happiness will spill over and affect your feelings too!

The next micro-action is not so simple. Caveat: this will be tough. Choose something that has always bothered you about your partner's behavior. The simpler, the better. It does not have to be something huge. Let's say it's the dishes—they never put them in the dishwasher.

The next part of this micro-action is to review and analyze your assumptions and emotions of that behavior. Your partner has left the dirty dishes there again, and you are angry. You feel that it is not your job to clean up after them. Why can't they carry their own weight?

Now you have an assumption that they don't share the workload evenly with you.

This experience has led to a bigger assumption attached to a small behavior. This assumption, that the relationship doesn't feel fair, is now more likely to transfer to other areas of your relationship, greatly affecting the happiness you feel with your partner. So, let's dig a bit deeper. Use your journal to document your behavior activity for the next micro-action.

Analyze how you would feel if your best friend, who is visiting from out of town, does the same behavior. Maybe you are saying: *But that's not the same thing. That's my best friend, and I don't have the same expectations.*

Recognize the difference in your feelings, expectations, and assumptions. This same emotional review can work for anyone who triggers you: a sibling, roommate, or co-worker.

Triggers are an unfortunate component of many relationships and the issues that surface with them. These include the power of people's words and how they make you feel, which are always connected to a larger experience that has little to do with what is happening in the present.

A typical example is, *Whenever my mother says [whatever], I know it is going to upset me.* This is a trigger; even if the circumstances change and the intention is different, your reaction will likely be the same as it has been every time you have had this experience. Triggers often arise more from the stories you tell yourself than from the intention of the person delivering the information.

It is most important that you realize that it is your assumption of the experience and not the experience itself is triggering you.

Changing your feelings associated with the triggers is a micro-action that leads to great power. But changing your feelings isn't an easy task. Practicing internal reflection that includes understanding the root of the assumption and its associated emotions, and then allowing yourself to explore where your focus goes when you are triggered, will help you to identify and process unresolved trauma and allow you to experience not just happiness, but freedom.

Gradually, you can practice separating the emotion from the behavior. This allows you to take back control over a situation where you previously felt powerless.

With your internal reflection, ask yourself this: Does the behavior create an impact on other parts of your relationship? This does not mean that the rationalization for why you felt those things will go away. This is important. This micro-action focuses on the emotion you get in association with the behavior, not the behavior itself necessarily. It is important to know how you would feel about it if your friend did it versus your partner. Try to realize how different your feelings can be about the same behavior.

The second step of this exercise is that when you see this materialize—in our example, when your partner leaves their plate beside the sink—don't engage with them. Your micro-action is no action.

Don't discuss it with them; don't acknowledge it at all. Try to avoid any emotions. Focus on something entirely unrelated. Try to imagine that it wasn't your significant other who did it, that it was your friend, so there is (hopefully) neutrality attached to the behavior—no guilt, anger, frustration, pain, or disappointment.

It does not mean that the behavior is right or wrong; it just means that, at this time, you are going to avoid addressing it. All the feelings that go along with it are what you are trying to neutralize.

Document in your journal each time you experience the behavior and your assumptions about it. The important part of this micro-action is your ability to separate yourself from the emotions attached to the experience. This is not going to be easy, but recognize that you can do this.

Once you have achieved small wins in this area, feel free to take on more, but keep the actions to micro-actions! If you take on something too big, you will fail.

Now that you have at least achieved neutrality with regard to this behavior, you can try to communicate to your partner what a modified behavior would mean to you. This is when you use the power of language. Remember, words carry powerful messages. The words you use won't only affect how you feel but also your ability to breathe fresh life into your relationship.

The goal isn't to hurt or criticize; it is to find a resolution so that you can experience more happiness with the person you love. Together, you could modify the behavior.

Please note that modifying the behavior is not essential. The essential part is modifying your assumption of the behavior. How you frame this experience is what leads to feelings of unhappiness. Only you have the power to change that.

This does not mean that the behavior is unimportant; it is that no emotion is attached to it. It is about knowing what things are important to carry and which ones can be let go.

The first time you try these micro-actions, expect to feel silly, but with effort and persistence, you will be rewarded. When you approach a concern without emotion, the other person won't feel attacked and become defensive; they will be more likely to listen and engage.

MORE PRACTICE

Creating a vision for where you want to go in your relationship is crucial, just like in all the other areas of your life. This is how you determine where you need to focus and how to implement micro-actions to improve your relationship.

As with your relationships with your siblings or parents, creating a continuum with your significant other is a valuable micro-action. What did the best of times look like? What did the worst of times look like? Now imagine what the absolute worst would be and what the absolute best would be.

What special micro-action could you do each day for your partner? A morning kiss? Use your journal to document a list of three to five possible micro-actions you can take right now. Whatever you choose, do it!

The next micro-action is journaling where you can make more time for your partner and relationship. Some of those things will be recurring, and others will be one-time events. Feel free to dream big for the future and include weekends away as well as recurring social times together for when you're ready to take on bigger commitments.

For now, a micro-action as simple as choosing one specific time of day that you set aside for your partner is good enough to get you started.

AMPLIFYING MICRO-ACTIONS:
UNDERSTANDING THE LOVE LANGUAGES

There are five love languages, and while most of us appreciate all of them, one of them likely has a greater impact on you than the others. This is your "primary" love language. This is true for your partner as well. A helpful way to identify their love language is to observe how they express love to others, as people often give love in the way they most enjoy receiving it.

Touch

Touch is a basic survival and safety need. However, each person interprets this in different ways. You've probably heard people say, "She's a hugger," or maybe, "I'm not one for hugs." Even those who may choose to avoid public touch receive touch in other ways: From a significant other, from a pet, or from less-intense types of contact like a handshake, eye contact, or a shoulder brush.

Most people fall somewhere between both extremes. Whatever it is for you, the point is that people need physical contact with other human beings to feel safe and loved.

So, how can you deliver micro-actions that offer some form of daily touch to your partner?

As a challenge, try to add to what you are already doing. Make it a natural physical encounter with your partner. This is not a sexual encounter; it is just a simple physical encounter. Something like brushing the hair off their forehead, giving their shoulders a massage, or even holding hands. Document the one micro-action you already do for them, and then think of one more you could add. Remember, this is not the thing they do for you—this is something you initiate.

Let's look at some micro-actions you can start with. Starting at the far end of the scale with the person who has hardly any physical touch with their partner, find the one token of affection that feels okay for you. It may be something simple like giving them a hug goodnight or a pat on the head. There may be a micro-action that feels very insignificant that you can do for now and gradually increase to something greater as you both become more comfortable with the touch.

Another approach is to make the touch entertaining rather than sexual, which may take some pressure off. Tickling is an easy way to do that.

Maybe you can increase the touch component through an existing task. Holding the tools for them, helping them with their jacket, or handing them a towel all connect you physically with your partner and allow you to start taking micro-actions to give rise to feelings of compassion, affection, and ultimately happiness. Be conscious of your partner's comfort level; you don't want to overstep their boundaries, but you can avoid this by discussing it with them first.

Document your thoughts about this challenge in your journal. What micro-actions do you currently do for your partner? What are you going to add to your daily touch routine?

Acts of Service

The second kind of acknowledgment is a micro-action that feels like a favor or an act of service. If you live in a frosty climate, it might be starting their car for them in the winter or doing a chore that is normally listed as theirs.

Doing favors is all about your individual household and the division of tasks. Sometimes the simplest micro-actions are the easiest to offer assistance with. Sometimes, you will need to make it clear you are doing them a favor, but mostly, you want to be able to do the micro-action and not need the validation that you have done it. This won't be easy, but that is the objective. Like physical touch, think of a micro-action you do now and a micro-action you will add to that routine.

Quality Time

The third form of acknowledgment is most easily described as quality time; however, this is more than just being with someone physically. It is about being fully present when you are with them and giving them your undivided attention.

The time should be spent doing an activity of their choice. This should not be something you have wanted to do or always do together. You'll find that this is likely an activity that you have resisted participating in that they have expressed interest in before. Maybe this micro-action looks like asking your partner if you can join in on their hobbies.

In this situation, you must be a silent observer, complaint-free and comment-free, and truly open-minded to learn about something they love! This might be a big challenge, so start small; consider watching their favorite TV show.

Micro-actions that involve doing tasks together might double up and be a way to increase your time together. Two-person jobs can be folding the laundry, doing the dishes, walking the dog, and even taking out the trash.

Take the time while doing these tasks together to find out about the other person and what is on their mind. Plan one little question as part of the micro-action, but try to make it a specific one that allows for an open response. So instead of asking, "How was your day?" try something more like: "How is the progress on your current project going? Are you on schedule?"

Maybe, in the beginning, the only micro-action you can find time to do together is to watch the late-night news, but take a moment to ask them about their impression of the broadcast and share your impression with them. Make the focus their comments, not yours.

Next, you want to work toward finding a micro-action you can do weekly, like having dinner out, going to a movie, taking a Sunday afternoon hike, or maybe making a Saturday brunch together. Whatever it is that you can think of, it should be a micro-action that you can do each week and that you both enjoy doing.

You can work on something larger once you can consistently stack these micro-actions.

If at first you try to dedicate a whole night of the week to the micro-action, you may sabotage your success. In the beginning, you may find that you can only manage the micro-action once a month. This is also okay. Whatever it is, you must recognize the objective: being one hundred percent in the moment's magic with your partner. No distractions, no texting, and no multitasking!

When these micro-actions have stacked up, and you feel you and your partner are happier, start envisioning the bigger picture. Annually, maybe you want to plan a weekend away. If not, be a tourist in your own town. Give your kids to someone else for the weekend—offer to do the same for them as an exchange. Have your home to yourselves.

The list is endless. You just need to make these micro-actions your priority and not let anything get in the way.

In your journal, chart where you currently are and then decide where you would like to be. From there, you can plot the micro-actions that will bring you closer to happiness.

Gifts

The next form of acknowledgment is gifts. This is one of the most common micro-actions to acknowledge another person.

This doesn't always need to be something you've bought and wrapped. A gift can be a micro-action as simple as an extra treat hidden in their lunch or their favorite item of food added to the shelf in the kitchen. Micro-actions that involve something they'd enjoy make people feel special.

For example, one person brings a grocery-store bouquet home. The other brings a grocery-store bouquet with additional flowers they understand are your favorite type and in colors to match your home. The second delivery's thoughtfulness acknowledges the gift's receiver more than the first one.

However, it is important to note that for those who place little value in receiving gifts, both deliveries would be equal. The extra thought will likely be lost on them, so it is important to know how your partner reacts to gifts before you use this as a micro-action.

And remember, you are not giving the gift with the expectation of receiving a gift or being praised for it. The micro-action is for your partner to show them how you feel.

Use your journal to document whether you think your partner's love language is gifts. How does your partner usually respond to gifts? What types of gifts do you usually get for your partner? What types of gifts could you get for your partner in the future?

Words

Another great way to acknowledge your partner is through your words. People speak to one another constantly, but finding ways to verbally acknowledge one another is not as natural.

Hearing that someone thinks you did a good job, being told you look nice, being congratulated for your success, or hearing words of thanks for your efforts are gifts for people whose love language is words. These micro-actions can also be written words: the gift of a note or a handwritten card.

Remember, words carry powerful messages. You may often try to say something nice about someone at a significant time, like when they have dressed up for a special occasion. However, you likely don't acknowledge how they look every other day.

Words have the power to significantly impact the lives of those around you. For those you love, realize that micro-actions that include kind words as they are leaving for work or when they come home can be very important to how they feel and experience happiness in the relationship.

Consider the difference between "Have a great day" and "I will be thinking of you today. I am confident you'll do well on that presentation." Or the difference between "Welcome home" and "So glad to see you. Thanks for all the time you spend supporting our family." Of course, it takes a bit more time to think of the extra kind words and have them be authentic. But when you are gifting this to your partner and showing them your love, isn't the extra time worth it?

Use your journal to reflect on some of the micro-actions you take to use your words to affirm your partner and how you might modify them. Write down the things you routinely say. Now, what micro-action will you include to amplify how they experience your love through your words?

FRIENDS

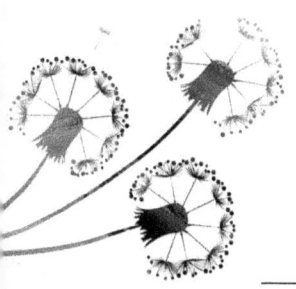

> *Lots of people want to ride with you*
> *in the limo, but what you want is*
> *someone who will take the bus with you*
> *when the limo breaks down.*
> — Oprah Winfrey

Before diving into your friendships, remember to start with the "Continuum Tool" to help you reflect on what you are moving away from and toward in this area. The scenarios that you generate using the tool will help you connect with the emotions associated with each situation. These emotions become the motivation needed to propel you away from the pain of the worst-case situation and toward the pleasure of the best-case situation to reprioritize your friends in your life. It is through these intentional micro-actions that you cultivate greater happiness.

By getting a better idea of the best- and worst-case scenarios, you will also be able to outline your goal for friends. Determining what this goal is will be your first micro-action. You can then use this larger goal to help you create smaller, more manageable micro-actions that can be incorporated into your life with far more ease. Remember to refer to "The Importance of Goals and Creating a Plan" in Part One for creating a plan for success, and

remember to download the "Goals," "Scheduling," and "Habits" resources from *nancysfreetools.com* to dive more deeply. Through these intentional micro-actions, you will build momentum and create a life that brings you happiness.

HOW DO YOU DEFINE FRIENDSHIP?

Friends can be a valuable treasure. Friends can be your siblings, people you've known your whole life, or people you meet and instantly sense a connection with.

How can you value these people? How can you give them appropriate time and consideration without compromising your happiness in other areas of your life?

Most people are lucky enough to have multiple friends, so the micro-actions in this chapter apply to all your friendships, old and new. This work can take a while, so start with the friendships that are the most important to you or the ones that feel the most in need of attention.

A helpful micro-action to start with in your friendships is to find out from your friends whether they view the friendship the same way you do. Has anything changed for them over the years? Do you have expectations of them that they don't have of you? This is particularly valuable if you feel you give more in friendships than you receive.

This conversation might seem awkward at first, but you can make it easier by starting with a positive statement about how much you appreciate the friendship. For example, you could say something like, "I love our special time together each month, and am so glad we do this together." Then, follow-up with a question, for example, "Do you do this activity with anyone else? or "Would you be open to adding something new to our routine, like a movie night?" This approach will help open the conversation and give you insight into how they perceive the friendship.

When you feel an emotion about how a friend has responded to you in a particular situation, identify what you are feeling and check in with your own emotions to determine if you are creating a story in your head. What assumptions have you made about this friendship, and what emotions are these assumptions creating? Where did these assumptions come from?

Understanding what experiences led you to have these assumptions and why the emotions associated with these assumptions are often unhelpful will allow you to make small changes that lead to more happiness in your relationships with your friends.

If you rely on your friendships to fill the unmet needs of your childhood or your partner, you often show up in friendships as needy and dependent—which can make it difficult for you to sustain friendships and can result in friendships that feel empty. Remember, you can find happiness when you focus on what you can control and take the necessary micro-actions that allow you to be responsible for your own life, including meeting your own unmet needs.

Doing the work to understand yourself better will allow you to release your friends from the responsibility you placed on them to take care of you or to make you happy. Only you can do that!

Do you remember your first friend? Perhaps it was your best friend from childhood or school days. This relationship was likely an easy relationship because the friendship existed for the sake of friendship, and there weren't any other expectations outside of that.

This sort of friendship is usually born of circumstance; you're in the same place at the same time. You may have lived close to one another, or your parents were friends. Many people won't even remember how they met their first friends. For others, the memory may be crystal clear. Whether you remember it or not, you know that you found yourself spending time together, sharing what you had in common, and that was enough.

In your youth, you probably had a lot of time to devote to your friendships and always made time for your friendships. But as we move into adulthood, budgeting our time may become tough. Most friends end up playing second fiddle to families, jobs, or significant others. In your adult years, a conscious effort must be made to maintain these friendships.

Do some inward reflection now and ask yourself where your focus on your friendships lies. How different do your friendships look now than when you were young?

Some friendships must be relatively strong to survive the long lapses between contact. Many things pull you away from your friends, and many of these seem completely reasonable. But, if you're honest with yourself, maintaining your friendships is often your least important priority, which might greatly contribute to the absence of happiness in your life.

People with honest and authentic relationships are happier and are more suited to improving other areas of their lives. Maintaining strong friendships provides amazing support through many of life's highs and lows and helps you survive the sideswipes that will come your way. Based on my own personal experience, I truly believe my friends have emotionally saved me countless times. They are the glue that holds my life together, and I could never imagine facing life without them.

Take a few minutes to engage in a journaling micro-action, reflecting on what made a close friendship work when you could give it a lot of attention so you know where your focus needs to shift to improve your relationships with your friends now. What values do you appreciate in your friends? Are these values that you embody in your friendships?

ASSESSING FRIENDSHIPS AND IMPRESSIONS OF THEM

How do you assess a friendship and determine how much happiness it brings you? If you want to develop an existing friendship further, build a new friendship, or strengthen one that has changed over time, then first reflect on what that friendship looks like and what friendship means to you.

The next micro-action you will take is to use the "Brain Warm-Up" tool in the Friends folder, available at *nancysfreetools.com*. The questions are designed to help you explore your emotions regarding your current friendships.

Friendships are in constant motion, and your view of them at any one time will be different, so happiness in this area is not simply attained but is worked on as it evolves.

Now that you have completed that micro-action, as with any reflective activity, hopefully you have gained insight into yourself and your friendship. This is a good time to make a few notes in your journal.

Think about this: If this is not an equal relationship, why are you continuing to be a part of it? Are you doing it out of obligation, habit, fear of being alone, or the age-old belief that something will change?

Maybe you are taking more than you're giving. Maybe you get a lot out of the relationship despite giving little or nothing to it.

If it is not equal, then determine the top three or four reasons why you are continuing with the friendship and make a note of those. If it is equal, great; list the top three or four qualities you take away when you leave that coffee date or phone call. Do you feel happy after that exchange?

Describe what you are feeling. Do you always feel the same way? Try to figure out if this feels like a friendship that opens the door toward more happiness or whether it is lacking. Are you looking forward to the next time you are together, or do you feel you need to recharge before you do it again? Do you feel this friendship honors reciprocity?

These are not easy questions to ask. There is no such thing as a balance that meets all your needs because life is messy. People are messy. Friendships are messy! If you aren't willing to ask yourself these uncomfortable questions about your friendships, you will never be able to do the work required to bring more happiness into your friendships.

A lot of the time, people report that they do things on auto-pilot. You meet with the girls once a week to have coffee, but what exchange happens? Why repeat this activity? Is this time spent because you believe that eventually, somehow, this activity will lead to happiness? Maybe you go and play basketball on Saturday mornings with friends. Do you do this for physical activity, or is there something more that you get from or give to this relationship?

Practice internal reflection when asking yourself these questions. Do you experience the magic of being in the present with these friends? Or are you watching the clock to see when it's time to leave?

Reflect on frequency. Do you wish that you could spend more time with these friends? What would you have to give up to do this activity more frequently? Would that be worth it?

Remember, you are trying to determine whether the minutes and hours you spend with your friend or friends are minutes that you spend exactly as you choose to spend them and feel good about. You are making a conscious choice about how you spend your time.

CHOICE IS EMPOWERING

Choice is one of the most empowering pursuits human beings can aspire to. When you choose to do something, you take control of your life. This is how you find the strength and determination to follow through with whatever you set your mind to.

If you do something out of obligation or responsibility, the strength and determination to see it through is not the same as when you truly choose to do it. The activity will be the same in both scenarios, but your response will be radically different.

Getting to a point in your life where all your micro-actions are choices is the objective. The knowledge that you are making a choice and the feeling of control will allow you to experience more self-mastery and ultimately more happiness. The more intention behind your micro-actions, the more they will feel like authentic decisions, and the more authentic your decisions, the more satisfied and fulfilled you will ultimately feel.

When you look at other components of your life and try to compare the time you spend in different areas, you can better rationalize the disproportionate amount of time you may be giving to some friendships. This work is challenging and easier to do with someone who can be objective and help you reflect on your feelings.

There are likely few friends or family members who can be truly objective allies. Professionals can offer more focused support, like a coach or a support group working toward a similar objective.

BUILDING FRIENDSHIPS

There is a good chance you have been so busy that you haven't thought much about building friendships. Being wrapped up in the busy lives of your children, moving, or being out of the workforce and detached from workplace relationships means your friendships may be sparse and poorly developed.

You may not have anyone that you consider a close friend.

This next micro-action is designed to help you explore what is involved in assembling your friend-building skills so that you can form supportive relationships that offer you guidance through life.

There is significant value in being part of a sincere friendship with a similar perspective or life experience. This person may have children of similar ages, be part of the same religious or cultural group, or even be part of your work environment, but above all, this person is someone you trust and can relate to. Often, this person knows a lot about you.

This kind of friendship is likely more common in your high school or college days when you have time to learn about one another. It is a bit more challenging to build later in life. Building on friendships is the easiest place to focus if you have been lucky enough to maintain lifelong friendships. In other cases, start fresh and build new friendships; it takes thoughtfulness, time, and energy to get to a point where they can bring genuine happiness into your life.

If you don't have this person in your life, still read through this section, as you may gain insight into ways to bring this into your life.

In the beginning, your micro-actions may include looking for a circle of friends and then later, within that circle, finding one or two that you connect to more easily. This may start from a micro-action like joining a school-based project with other parents or adding a social component to a sports activity you participate in, like going to get a cold drink or coffee after the basketball game, golf round, or yoga class.

What is the value of a friendship circle or a support group? You may find support in other spaces. Each social group may support you differently, filling an area the others can't.

Your partner offers support but offers you something different from what your siblings can offer. The insight a good friend can provide differs greatly from what you might receive from your sister or mother. Friends have a way of knowing what you need to hear, even when you don't want to hear it—and we are usually more willing to receive it from them!

Start this work by doing some internal reflection. Explore the components of your life where you currently have a social circle. Work, high-school friends, other parents, teammates from recreational sports, and friends acquired through religious gatherings all count.

Your true interests bring you close to finding a group of like-minded people. In some cases, it will be your kids who bring you together. You may have chosen a particular school, and others who have chosen a similar school may have the same beliefs. You may share child-care tips and the framework for creating deeper bonds. A social event with these people might be a safe place to start when considering building new friendships.

Remember—you must be willing to adapt and be intentional with your micro-actions! Building new friendships might be the best way to start practicing actions that promote happiness in your life. Whatever opportunity you have to extend a friendship request, take a risk and try.

Another option is to draw on your high-school interests. If you were a track star in high school, maybe you don't do track anymore now that you have three kids, but maybe you still manage to run occasionally, and a running group might be what you want to look for. Bonding over a common interest is one of the easiest ways to connect.

Taking bold micro-actions that bring you closer to real connection and allow your walls to slowly come down will allow you to build deeper and more meaningful friendships.

Happiness favors the brave. Most people work particularly hard to mask their vulnerabilities, so taking micro-actions to meet new people, trusting that wholesome friendships will be built from these roots, and being more open to the possibilities that come with these friendships will allow you to cultivate friendships with depth, integrity, and happiness.

Find ways to be more open, trusting, and vulnerable like being honest about your intentions, letting people know why your friendships have failed in the past, or admitting that you're lonely. Allowing yourself to be seen and accepted for this vulnerability will give you the courage to turn your micro-actions into enriching relationships that lead to greater satisfaction in life and happiness.

This may take some practice. Keeping it simple without too many requirements is also important—your life is busy enough, and even the best intentions can fall apart. Remember to be kind to yourself and patient with the process. It takes repetition and practice, so don't give up—it's worth the effort.

It's time to practice internal reflection. Use your journal to write down which micro-actions you could take and who you might include. Once you have taken these steps, return to this chapter. Did you follow through with the plans? Was it a positive experience? What will you do next?

As you study yourself more and more, you may find that there is value in having friends who are your senior, who are your junior, and friends who have children older or younger than yours. Sharing with friends in different phases of life allows you to gain insight into the next season and allows you to share and encourage those who are new to the experiences you have mastered. There is security in knowing what the challenges are likely to be and that there is a path to follow that will lead you out that others have successfully traveled.

It is also valuable to share your own experiences and challenges and support with the group following behind you, to those who are coming into the phase you are leaving, giving you a chance to be a mentor and guide someone else. Another approach to consider might be to find someone who is radically different from you and can open your eyes to another way of seeing the world. You may find that what you discover is a whole new way of experiencing happiness.

SOCIALIZATION

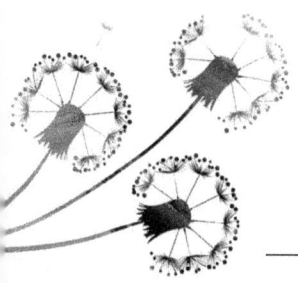

*The only work that will ultimately bring
any good to any of us is the work of
contributing to the healing of the world.*
— MARIANNE WILLIAMSON

Before diving into socialization, remember to start with the "Continuum Tool" to help you reflect on what you are moving away from and toward in this area. The scenarios that you generate using the tool will help you connect with the emotions associated with each situation. These emotions become the motivation needed to propel you away from the pain of the worst-case situation and toward the pleasure of the best-case situation to reprioritize socialization in your life. It is through these intentional micro-actions that you cultivate greater happiness.

By getting a better idea of the best- and worst-case scenarios, you will also be able to outline your goal for socialization. Determining what this goal is will be your first micro-action. You can then use this larger goal to help you create smaller, more manageable micro-actions that can be incorporated into your life with far more ease. Remember to refer to "The Importance of Goals and Creating a Plan" in Part One for creating a plan for success, and remember to download the "Goals," "Scheduling," and "Habits" resources from *nancysfreetools.com* to dive more deeply. Through these intentional micro-actions, you will build momentum and create a life that brings you happiness.

THE VALUE OF EXPANDING YOUR EXPERIENCES

Healing the world. Does this resonate with you? Do you feel some responsibility to make the world a better place?

I have always been surrounded by people who care about their impact on the world, everything from littering to the kind of cars they drive. However, I do not profess to be well-informed on world repair issues. My perspective comes from shifting my focus away from myself and toward humanity: If I make a mess, I should clean it up. If I am having a negative impact on the world, I should try to change that.

So how does my connection with the world relate to my social connections? I am sure it is easy for you to connect with the idea that we are social creatures and that we do better when we work together than when we try to go in alone!

Independence is an admired quality. But reality is different—we are not successful when we try to function independently. Not only are we better when we work together with other people, but we also improve our world when we work in balance with our environment. So, as you explore this next area, think about how these concepts are intertwined and if you can better understand how interconnecting them serves you personally. How does connecting with others heal the world?

SOCIALIZING

Socialization promotes the idea that allowing bigger circles of people into your life is important. A group of couples and a network of friends with similar interests will complement and enhance your existing social network, expanding your opportunities for experiencing happiness and taking micro-actions to heal the world. This bigger social circle might include your spiritual community, your place of work, or the places where you volunteer your time.

So, what does socialization look like?

A starting micro-action might look like putting a friend group together and extending the invitation to include their plus ones. Keep the invitation very relaxed. Also, make sure it's casual, with no clear arrival or departure time and no participation requirements, but make sure it includes some mixing time—this is usually easiest around food.

Once this event has unfolded successfully, make the event more structured—like sharing the organization of the next dinner event for six to eight people with others in the circle.

Typically, the argument is: *I don't have a circle of friends with which my significant other and I hang out. I have my circle of friends that I hang out with, and they have theirs. It doesn't usually work out when we ask significant others to join us.*

It may not always work out perfectly. However, there is still some value in doing activities like these that allow for a different kind of socialization. Having a planned activity makes these events go more smoothly.

In past generations, this type of socialization was more common. Social groups like bridge clubs were common in my grandmother's generation. These couples would spend scheduled evenings together playing bridge. For you, it might look like board games or poker night. No matter what it is, most people feel it's hard to take the micro-actions necessary to keep this kind of socialization a part of their routines.

It takes work, but it's always worth it. The more casual the event, the more successful it will be. The less pressure everyone feels, the more they are likely to want to repeat it. Don't get caught up in overplanning or having everything "perfect." Remember, it is about community—and these micro-actions aim to help you be happier in the ordinary moments, not the perfect ones.

Socializing as a couple will provide you with more shared experiences and help you understand how others navigate social situations. Human beings are designed to learn how to be in relationships from watching others be in relationships, so there is immense value in spending time with other people in social spaces. Try to keep the number of people involved to about six people. The small group works better because it allows you to actually talk.

TIME—HOW IS IT POSSIBLE?

Instead of finding time away from your family for socialization, find an activity you can do together with other couples and families and get everyone involved. These don't have to be grand gestures to be fun. It's consistency that counts, and this fills your cup on a regular basis.

Pick something you can do together that can keep the kids busy; that way, the conversation isn't likely to be strained. Remember, creating a kid-friendly space doesn't need to be complicated! One idea could be to create a fun dinner in your home. Another idea could be to create a movie night for your kids in a separate space in your home that allows you to have them close by but not part of the adult event. You can do this by using your computer, a projector, and a white sheet on a garage wall! Simply add the kids, their pillows, sleeping bags or blankets, and popcorn, and you're all set!

If this feels like a micro-action that can help get you started in the area of socializing, invite three or four couples over for a dinner club. Each couple contributes a component of the meal, minimizing cost, and the event itself can change venues. The biggest trick to this kind of event is to make it enough fun that people will want to do it again.

By socializing as a couple, you typically interact differently. Socializing is something you may have done a lot more of when you were dating. Maybe you are a bit out of practice.

Consider the experience of purely socializing—interacting with others without any agenda. I remember when my children were in school, many of my "social" experiences revolved around school events, often tied to fundraisers or activities my children were involved in. In most cases, we parents were organizers or volunteers with specific responsibilities, which sometimes left our partners feeling unnecessary or excluded. While these events offered some level of social interaction, they didn't truly fulfill the need for meaningful socializing as a couple.

If the gatherings you have been part of more recently have required that one or both of you have had tasks or duties, those who are more involved may feel more connected, while others may feel left out. Striving for a more balanced level of participation can enhance the social experience for both of you.

What micro-action can you take to start practicing socializing as a couple? How will this benefit your relationship and your family? You may even end up having some genuine fun while you are doing it!

Maybe the first micro-action in this area looks like getting tickets to performing arts, theater, or musical entertainment. Maybe it's something else. What matters here is taking micro-actions that you can do together where both of you will be able to participate fully, enhancing your opportunity to experience more happiness—together as a couple.

LONGEVITY AND SOCIAL CONNECTEDNESS

Recently, there has been increasing conversation about longevity and happiness. COVID-19 has brought much of the research to the forefront as we have all had more time to reflect on our priorities. Most studies have come to the conclusion that while exercise and diet are still very important factors in longevity, social connectedness has a significant part to play.

Your work might seem to be the most important factor in your ability to provide for yourself and your family, and it may be incredibly fulfilling. But no matter who you are or the kind of work you do, finding true happiness and fulfillment is pretty unlikely if you don't create a social network for yourself.

Connecting and socializing as a couple is part of this happiness. If you truly want to reap the benefits of micro-actions, start right where you are—in your home, with the people you love, doing the things that make you happy. It doesn't get simpler than that.

Most people lead incredibly busy lives and find it hard to make time to take these kinds of micro-actions. Even when you say you want to do something, it seems that your social life is never truly your focus.

Sometimes, the easiest way to start is to choose a holiday when you know people are more likely to be available or are willing to celebrate. That could be something like a religious holiday, historical holiday, national holiday, sporting event, or even a fun "Hallmark" theme day. It could also be the celebration of a "half-birthday," completing a project at work, or a home renovation. Anything can be your excuse to create a celebration. Keep it easy and utilize micro-actions—and don't go over the top with decorations or the meal plan!

Now, practice some internal reflection. What are your thoughts on socializing? What do you currently do in this area? What micro-actions can you take to improve your social life? Having a social component in your life will enhance your life experience, relationships, and, ultimately, happiness.

SOCIAL CONSCIENCE AND VOLUNTEERING

Social conscience is tied to being social. This connection might not be obvious, but they are intertwined. Who you show up as in your social circle should include all the parts of who you are.

As much as you would like to resist your social environment shaping who you become, you can't escape the fact that who you surround yourself with influences how you show up in all areas of your life. Your community contribution has a similar impact on your social circles and can enhance your social experience—and provide tremendous opportunities for happiness.

By participating in your greater community and giving your time and expertise for the benefit of others, you not only enhance your community and the world in which you live but also benefit personally from the experiences. When you share your time and knowledge, you are fulfilling your greater purpose and serving others.

This might seem like an altruistic behavior, but it really is what makes us human and builds strong communities. Mutual support is the fabric of life in a community.

What do you give to your community? How do you participate in the world around you? What are you doing that affects the other humans in your immediate circle? Do you have a volunteer life?

When you speak to anyone who has been incredibly successful or well-known, and you ask them to compare the impact of their paid work to their volunteer work experiences, most speak highly of their volunteer experiences. So, what does a social contribution mean to you?

No matter where or when you find yourself reflecting on your purpose in the world, it often has something to do with other people. Your social contribution and your life's purpose are interconnected. No matter your profession or job, you can weave this work back to how this work supports your social contribution.

In some cases, this is very obvious, such as where the job serves a purpose for society. Typically, these jobs are considered to be part of the service industry. This could include sales, legal or financial services, healthcare, teaching, plumbers, gardeners, firefighters, government services, politicians, and armed forces. With such a broad vision, it might be hard to think of a position that couldn't be considered a service.

Once you see that most jobs provide a service, it is easier to understand how most jobs can contribute to society.

Take a "regular" job and think about how it provides social contribution and fulfillment. Understanding this concept can help focus and propel you toward your life's purpose and social contribution.

There are so many ways to give back to society through volunteering. You just need to determine the area you have a passion for, whether that's reading to young children, helping the elderly, working with teens, constructing homes, helping on school boards or in playgrounds, or the like.

The experiences you have in the moments of volunteering are so fulfilling that they will allow you to view your life differently and shift your perspective.

Most volunteers have a collection of life-changing experiences from their volunteer work. They are the kind of experiences that you hold onto forever. These are stories you tell your grandchildren, and what make up your legacy.

These truly are the real kind of micro-actions—small contributions that impact the world in a big way. They are the micro-actions that make you human. They are the times that allow you to be truly thankful for your opportunities and advantages. It takes effort to make the time, but many people will tell you that the effort is well worth the reward.

There are many local and national organizations where you can take micro-actions to volunteer your time. Local hospitals, schools, libraries, churches, and food distribution organizations are almost always looking for helpers. Even something simple will give you opportunities you would have otherwise missed.

Whether it is fundraising for a school or church group or spooning out soup at a local food bank, the opportunities are twofold (sometimes tenfold): One is that you are giving of yourself and sharing your skills with another group of human beings who most often are very grateful for what you can offer. The second component that most people don't consider is socialization.

When you work with others with the same goal in mind, there is a connection that is not easily replicated in other situations. The difference between the workplace and the volunteer space is that the latter lacks competition. Everyone is working for a common goal. There is no need to be better than anybody else.

In the regular workplace, competition is rewarded with income, accolades, and prestige; that does not happen in the volunteer workplace. When you remove the competitive component, what you have is just true altruism, and typically, the comradery you get from that experience is a taste of real happiness.

You may also find that you develop a special bond with others when you become involved in your religious communities or school communities. The comradery comes from a trusting space where you are all intentionally choosing micro-actions that lead to the betterment of that community, with common goals and with no personal agenda. The connections formed here are far more meaningful than many other social activities that we share.

If you currently aren't taking any micro-actions to be of service in your community, take a micro-action now. Go out and find something in your community. Look at the benefits you can both give and receive from volunteering. Time is often our excuse, but even an activity you only do annually can be a significant experience.

It's important to acknowledge that there is a benefit to volunteering—and see the positive impact it has on the lives of others and your own. Opening your world to the way other people live, recognizing how privileged you are, and seeing the resilience of people who have been through so much heartache will allow you to shift your focus back to what matters: Our shared humanity, the impermanence of life, and the love of the people around you.

This is how you reflect inwardly. This is how you use the power of your words to change narratives and shape your world. This is how you connect with your emotions to contemplate your life experiences and the assumptions you have drawn from them.

This is how you shift your focus to gratitude, to love, to mercy. This is how you find the ability to stand in the magic of the present moment and take brave micro-actions to open yourself up fully to experience true happiness.

A NOTE FROM ME TO YOU

By reading this book, you have empowered yourself to build a life where you intentionally practice happiness. At any time you can come back to this resource, and refer to any section where you need to do additional work. Use this book as a guide as you travel through different seasons of your life. Life is dynamic, and the way your world looks will change, so don't get comfortable. Rather, get skilled at adapting, at shifting focus, and at making an effort to put the "Happiness Practices" into motion and create the happiness you seek.

My greatest successes occur when I take on tasks that are attainable. This is why there is such a focus on micro-actions in the book. It really is the big things broken down into smaller, more manageable parts that allows me to change my world.

If you have more questions and want to dig deeper, connect with me! Subscribe to my YouTube channel or send me a message on Facebook and/ or Instagram. I'd love to hear from you!

But first, congratulate yourself on all the micro-actions you have taken to get this far. Reflect on your progress, reflect on everything you have overcome to stand in the magic of your life at this moment. Look around. You did this. Now let's do even more. Find out more at *nancyfreedman.com*.

ABOUT THE AUTHOR

Nancy Freedman's lifetime experience in healthcare shaped her passion for the power of personal development and inspired her journey as an educator, writer, and speaker. With nearly forty years as a registered nurse, her career spanned specialties where teaching was at the heart of her work, whether guiding parents in pediatric intensive care, empowering renal-failure patients in home dialysis programs, training healthcare professionals as a clinical IT specialist, or mentoring physicians in her role as Director of Medical Staff.

A natural teacher and communicator, Nancy has always been drawn to personal psychology, a fascination that started in her undergraduate studies and continues to inspire the work she does today. In 2022 she decided to take a very rough draft of a manuscript—born from her own experience of pain and powerlessness through grief, and the realization that happiness must come from within if it's to last—and turned it into more than just a legacy for her children. This is a formidable book that will educate, inspire, and guide readers toward self-discovery, personal growth, and genuine happiness.

Nancy's ability to break down complex topics into clear, attainable goals is evident in her writing, just as it is in her sought-after online classes. With her engaging storytelling, bold vulnerability, and practical tools, Nancy's work makes the shift from concept to action uncomplicated and accessible to all.

She is a dynamic speaker with an authentic presence, connecting with her audiences on a deeply personal level, fostering safe spaces that are enriching and empowering.

Beyond her professional expertise, Nancy's greatest gift is her ability to listen, learn, and uplift those around her. Whether through her writing, speaking, or social media presence, Nancy is on a mission to show others how they can take an active role in their own lives and discover a more meaningful sense of happiness—one micro-action at a time.

To connect with Nancy and learn more about her work, visit:
www.nancyfreedman.com.

www.ingramcontent.com/pod-product-compliance
Lightning Source LLC
Chambersburg PA
CBHW041628140626
46547CB00031B/1236